Rhythms and Cycles

*Sacred
Patterns
in
Everyday
Life*

Nancy Pauline Bruning

A Crossroad 8th Avenue Book
The Crossroad Publishing Company
New York

Human Basics^{SM}

The Crossroad Publishing Company
481 Eighth Avenue, Suite 1550
New York, NY 10001

Human Basics^{SM} is a service mark of
The Crossroad Publishing Company

LIBRARY OF CONGRESS CATALOGING-IN-PUBLICATION DATA
Bruning, Nancy.
Rhythms and cycles: sacred patterns in everyday life / by Nancy
Pauline Bruning.
p. cm.
"A Crossroad Eighth Avenue book."
Includes bibliographical references (p. 214)
ISBN 0-8245-1962-0
1. Religions.   I. Title.
BL85 .B84 2001
291.3—dc21
2001002152

Printed in the United States of America
Set in Janson

Designed and produced by SCRIBES BOOKS
Cover art © by Nancy Pauline Bruning

FIRST EDITION

1 2 3 4 5 6 7 8 9 10 04 03 02 01

This book is dedicated to Mom, the sweetest angel in heaven, if there is one.

*To what extent is a person held slave
to the environment, to the ancestry, to the
tricks of time? Are we pliable, receptive
entities, fertile with limitless possibilities
of the present and future, mere clay,
sculpted by messages that sprang
from a hidden, unknown past?*

—Mel Donalson, *River Woman*

More advance praise for
Rhythms and Cycles:

"Nancy Bruning's wonderful walk through world culture gives a clear and comprehensive incentive to try to get our rhythm back!"

—**Reverend Robert Cormier,** author of *A Faith That Makes Sense*

"In the hectic rush of the modern world, the cycles of life often become obscured. Nancy Bruning's Rhythms and Cycles *puts us back in touch with the wisdom of the ages. We should heed her message."*

—**Michael Castleman,** author of *The New Healing Herbs and Nature's Cures*

"We all need more structured ways to feel grounded in life and whether we incorporate traditional religious rituals to achieve this or we create our own spiritual paths, we each must find our own definite rhythm in life and yet leave the door open to new possibilities which might shake our balance a little but lift us to some higher level. Rhythms and Cycles *makes you aware of the need for the observance of the rhythms and sacred patterns in our lives."*

—**Latif Bolat,** Director of the Mevlevi Association of American Whirling Dervishes

"Clearly and beautifully written! This book is a strong reminder of the importance of finding solace, focus and serenity through the ritual and practice of the spiritual in our lives."

—**Rosa Lamoreaux,** recording artist, "Luminous Spirit"

"Spiritual life entails prayer, ritual, and meditation but mainly the daily experience of encountering God in word and in silence. Nancy Bruning projects this unique experience in Rhythms and Cycles *(which I read with great delight on Shabbath). . . . [A] book to be read and reflected upon."*

—**Rabbi Leon Klenicki,** Consultant for Interfaith Affairs, Anti-Defamation League

*"*Rhythms and Cycles *is a unifying celebration of the points where all the earth's peoples and religions are bound together by the same cycles of nature. A lively read!"*

—**Laeh Maggie Garfield,** author of *Sound Medicine*

Acknowledgements

No writer writes a book alone, and this one is no exception. First and foremost, I would like to thank my publisher, Gwendolin Herder for suggesting this book in the first place, and for giving me the opportunity to explore new fields of thinking and knowledge. My appreciation to my editor Barbara Ellis, for her unfailing enthusiasm, endless knowledge and gentle but firm guidance. I would especially like to thank all the people I spoke with and interviewed, for so graciously and generously sharing with me their thoughts, knowledge and time: John Ratti, editor at the Episcopal Church Center, who started me off in the right direction; Frank Tedeschi, managing editor of Church Publications

Company; Reverend Sharon Blackburn, senior minister and Peter Stoltfus, minister of music and organist at the Plymouth Church of the Pilgrims in Brooklyn; Reverend Robert Cormier, associate pastor at the St. Rose of Lima Parish in Newark, New Jersey; Rabbi Leon Klenicki, director of Interfaith Affairs of the Anti-Defamation League; Rachel McDermott, assistant professor of Asian and Middle Eastern cultures, Barnard College; Anand Mohan, associate professor of philosophy and religious studies, Queens College at CUNY; Rabbi Marcelo Bronstein, of B'nai Jeshurun in New York; Reverend Kobutsu Malone, Zen Buddhist priest in Ramsey, New Jersey and head of a nation-wide prison ministry; Irvin Ungar, former "pulpit" rabbi and current owner of Historicana Rare Books and Manuscripts; Omar Abunamous, assistant Imam at the Islamic Cultural Center in New York; Betty Roi, singer and Iyengar-style yoga instructor; Rosa Lamoreaux, soprano performer of sacred and other music; Latif Bolat, performer and composer of Turkish devotional music and music director of the Mevlevi Association of American Whirling Dervishes.

I would also like to thank Shaykha Fariha and Michael Harrison, leaders of the zikrs I attended in New York City, and the staff of Sufi Books that led me to them, as well as the other numerous houses of worship that welcomed me during the research for this project.

I could not have written this book without my friends of many faiths who encouraged me, read parts of the manuscript, accompanied me in the field and generally did what friends are supposed to do, in particular the divine Kathleen O'Reilly, Ronnie Himmel, Thomas Wolf, Lucy O'Flaherty, Stephen Joseph, Rosa Naparstek, Toby Heifitz, Brent Kohler, Cindy Servetnick, Estelle Ardell and Betty Straus.

Contents

Che lascia la via vecchia per la nuova,
so quell che perde e non sa quell che trova.

(Whoever forsakes the old way for the new
knows what he is losing, but not
what he will find.)

—Italian proverb

Preface

When I was a little girl growing up in Brooklyn, the borough of churches, I always knew where I was going to be on Sunday mornings: Sunday School. To this weekly ritual was eventually added the grown-up church service with its gorgeous music, the mysterious sacrament of the Eucharist, the sunlight streaming through the jewel-like stained glass windows. After church, my tiny family indulged in fresh-baked crusty rolls and crumb cake, with their yeasty, wheaty cinnamon fragrance and special Sunday aura. There were also two grand holidays—Easter Sunday, with the church dressed up with flowers and me dressed up in my new spring outfit; and Christmas, with its carols and candles and colorful Advent calendars with the fascinating little windows and doors that swung open and shut. These are mostly fond memories, but I grew to have too many questions and the clergy had too few answers.

Fast forward to the millennium. The little Lutheran girl has grown up. I've had two Jewish husbands whose families introduced me to a warmth, humor and liveliness that resonated in a different way than the church music, sunlight, etc. of my youth. I have survived a life-threatening disease and the deaths of more loved ones than I want to count. I have lived for a decade on the West Coast, where Eastern religions showed me new ways of seeing and being. Now back on the right side of the continent, I feel nostalgic for those trips to the bakery for crusty rolls on Sunday, the thrill of a spiffy new Easter outfit, a real Christmas tree with lights, the church choir. But surely it's not the rolls, the clothes, the tree themselves I long for—it's what they represent.

Today, my life is too often a fragmented, unpredictable blur. Like many self-employed people, there are no weekends, and the home "office" rarely shuts down at "normal" hours. This fractured fairy tale of a life is exciting, but it can also be draining physically, mentally and spiritually. Thanks to my work as a health writer, I have grown to feel respect and wonder at the many pathways that the body, mind and spirit influence each other. I have learned that living life on the edge is cool only if you know how to stay balanced and that true health goes beyond eating three healthy meals a day and exercising regularly. I have realized that religion and spirituality go deeper than my simple girlish memories. And I have come to believe that regularly observing and appreciating the rhythms and cycles that ground our spiritual traditions nourishes our spiritual selves with love, obligation and poetry. They are food for the soul.

—*Nancy Pauline Bruning*
September 2001, New York City

Introduction

To every thing there is a season, and a time to every purpose under the heaven: A time to be born, and a time to die; a time to plant, and a time to pluck up that which is planted.
—Ecclesiastes 3:1-2

It's hard to believe those timeless words were written thousands of years ago, especially if you are of the generation who remembers the long-haired Byrds, and their long-lived hit recording of a song based on those very lyrics. Yes, all of life—including our own—chugs along rhythmically in cycles. Cycles shape and give direction to our lives, to our relationships to each other, to nature and to our creator, whether we realize it or not.

In earlier times, when people lived closer to nature, they were probably more aware of this simple truth. Today we need to be reminded that rhythm applies to more than just the beat of the music on the radio, and there are other cycles besides the billing cycle of our credit cards. Life's essential patterns are everywhere, if we just pause to look, listen, feel and remember.

The rising and setting of the sun urges us out of bed and back in again. The blanket of snow giving way to a patch of golden daffodils lifts our spirits and tells us its time to put away those heavy, woolen winter clothes. The gurgling of digestive juices and the grumbling of our stomachs let us know when its time to eat and time to stop eating (except on Thanksgiving and Passover). In fact, every time we breathe in and breathe out we are experiencing the rhythmic changes that form the fabric of our existence on earth.

Since our belief systems are but mirrors of the needs and experiences of humanity, they too, weave their own exquisite temporal patterns: feasts, rituals, holy days, prayer times, sacred songs, chants and dances. Reminders of history and creators of sacred time, these patterns parallel the underlying rhythms of our day, week, month, year and lifetime. What do they mean? What is their purpose? Why would we still honor such age-old practices? Why rest on the Sabbath instead of shop or work to get ahead? Why mourn a death for eleven months? Why bless our food? Pray once, three times, five times every day? Make a pilgrimage?

"I have too much to do already! I can barely keep my PalmPilot updated," you say? "Now you want me to thank God each morning and night for all my blessings? You're thinking I should light the Sabbath candles every Friday? Gimme a break!"

That is exactly the point. In these hectic times such rituals and observances are more difficult to follow. But they are paradoxically needed more than ever.

In our technologically advanced societies we experience days and nights that are fractured and frantic, shaped by the relentless virtual ticking of a digital clock instead of the sublime music of the spheres. We distort daily rhythms, ignore yearly seasons and deny the reality of the last turn of the wheel of life. We seldom get together as a family (however you choose to define it) and seldom even eat a meal together, let alone pray together. Day after day goes by, its memory a mere blur of activity, angst, emptiness or boredom.

Whatever our religion or beliefs, it's time to pay closer attention to the sacred rhythms that pulse all around us. Rather than getting lost in the urgency and obligation of buying Christmas gifts or Seder ingredients, what if we could be present at every moment and savor the true meaning of these celebrations? Instead of trying to cram tons of activities into the weekend, what if we gave ourselves the gift of rest, a break from the rat race? In place of eating on automatic pilot, can we appreciate food anew after the abstention of Ramadan, Lent and Yom Kippur has whetted our appetites?

Granted, religious rituals can themselves be as meaningless and rote as doing a laundry, as rigidly regimental as an army drill, as numbingly dull as a bad sermon. Their value and significance depend on us and the circumstances. When we observe these traditions with due understanding and awe, we not only mark specific important events; we also more keenly feel the holiness of all moments. In setting aside time, we give a more graceful and coherent shape to that precious commodity. Observing such events and practices imparts a welcome perspective, stability and structure without (we hope) unyielding rigidity. With each prayer uttered, each holy meal eaten, each candle lighted, we reconnect with our roots, slow down, replenish and become more grounded. Our lives become richer, our religious beliefs rejuvenated. Ultimately we come closer to that state of grace in which we feel closer to nature, the core of life, humanity and God.

It has been said that religion exists because humans are afraid of death. Perhaps. It's possible to be also afraid of life, with all its trials and tribulations, its ups and downs, its unpredictability. By practicing religious rituals and observing spiritual traditions regularly, we may be adding a comforting layer of order, predictability and balance to our modern existence, which can seem so perilously chaotic and out of control. We learn that "This too shall pass . . ." In all religious traditions, sound melts into silence, movement settles into stillness, light diminishes toward darkness, fasting gives way to feasting, solitude gathers into community, mourning turns into celebration, youth grows into maturity and death leads to something beyond . . . and back again.

Thank God!

1. *Roots and Roles*

*I have discovered that there is a pattern, larger and
more beautiful than our short vision can weave.*

—Julia Seton, *By a Thousand Fires*

*The spirit like the body can
be strengthened and developed
by frequent use.*

—Wassily Kadinsky

It's a crisp, snowy night in the middle of winter. Feet crunch on the cold, slippery, white covering dusted with a layer of brownish black soot. The short days of pale thin sunlight, the long shivery nights, the commercialism of Christmas dampen the city's spirits. Heavy waterproof, skid-proof boots walk up the steps of a modest historic twilight-darkened church in Brooklyn. Inside a small light illuminates a young organist and his music. Quiet prevails amidst the hushed murmurs of the congregation. Softly, slowly, the organist begins playing a variation of "O Come, O Come, Emmanuel." The walls, the pews, the people reverberate as the deep tones build and fill the air. A pause; then, the tender, ethereal voice of a child pierces the dark singing, "Drop down ye heavens from above, and let the skies pour forth righteousness: let the earth be fruitful, and bring forth a Savior." Hearts burst with joy at the sound of her voice and the meaning of the words. Thus begins Plymouth Church of the Pilgrims' Advent service.

As the service continues, the choir progresses from a remote location in the darkened church, and the space gradually becomes more illuminated. Between appropriate readings, lessons and music, the choir alternately proceeds and pauses until it reaches the full light of the sanctuary. There is meaning in this movement and stillness, light and darkness, sound and silence. In the formal sanctuary of the church, worshipers have emerged from the singularity of their own lives to worship as one body, to be in unity with each other and with their God. In this, there is celebration and mourning, solitude and community and hopes about death and beyond.

Halfway around the globe a group of Australian aborigines stand in the sere heat of a barren landscape. Their bare feet kick up tiny clouds of reddish dust as they walk and walk and walk the same paths their ancestors walked for millennia. They dance and sing to the sounds of the musical instrument, the didgeridoo, singing the sounds and making the movements their ancestors made when they sang and danced the world into existence. They use sound and movement to enter the Dreamtime, the ancient sacred time and place that is the eternal moment of all creation. In this sun-soaked ancient gathering, as in the snow-powdered Advent service—as in all rituals—things are more than they seem.

There is "rich symbolism" in the advent of Christ's birth, says Peter Stoltzfus, the church's minister of music, and in the progression of the choir. For example, "the movement of our own spiritual journeys toward God, and our movement to the foot of the cross as we experience redemption." And that's just the tip of the iceberg: this Christian rite embodies many of the themes found in the rhythms and cycles of life and mirrored in all wisdom traditions. When the Catholic priest raises the cup of wine to bless it before the Eucharist, when the Torah is passed around during a Sabbath service, when the five-times-a-day prayer is recited and enacted at the mosque, when the Hindu makes an offering of incense to the deity of her choice, when the gong calls the Buddhist to a sitting meditation, when the aborigine retraces his ancestor's footsteps—for the faithful these acts, too, evoke unfathomable layers of meaning and beliefs. Why do we perform these rites? Where do these rites come from? What forms do they take? And most importantly: Are they still relevant today?

MAKING FAITH REAL

Why pray, chant, recite scripture or meditate? Why take part in a pilgrimage, go to weekly services at a church, temple or mosque? This is like asking why we believe in any particular faith. Or in God. Rituals are the physical expression of our beliefs. These activities counterbalance the harrowing uncertainty of everyday life. They calm and shelter us in a world that is often without reason or peace, and that can shatter us without warning.

Religious rituals have many forms and goals, but one purpose overall: to express, uphold and further the beliefs of our religion, and to comfort us as we make our spiritual journey through life. Religious beliefs are by nature nonmaterial—elusive, slippery, hard to hold. They are difficult to express. Rituals and other practices are the bricks and mortar of spirituality. They are where spirit and substance meet. Since we are both material and nonmaterial beings, but mostly spending more time in the material world, repeating religious practices over and over makes our beliefs more concrete. Hearing the same stories and the same lessons, singing the same songs, praying the same prayers, over and over again, until they have sunk deep into the soul, help strengthen faith and make it more real—within ourselves, and in the world at large. Thus, they dangle before us the delicious possibility common to all faiths: some form of immortality and union with the Supreme Creator.

Although the concept of rhythms and cycles is important in all religions, in Hinduism, they are not just "important," they form the very foundation of the entire Hindu belief system. Just as Christianity would be hard pressed to justify its existence without the divinity of Christ, Hinduism requires the concept of the turning wheel of life that repeats over and over. For the Hindu, time is cyclical, as is existence.

As Rachel McDermott, assistant professor of Asian and Middle Eastern cultures at Barnard College explains it, "Nothing is static. In fact, the word for the world, *samsara*, comes from a Sanskrit word which means 'to move.'" This universe of constant motion includes the idea of reincarnation, of dying and being reborn again and again until you experience the *moksha* of liberation and are finally able to jump off the cycle of life and become one with Brahman. Movement is the nature of life, but movement is also the problem with life. "And the solution is to break out of the cycle of movement—to quiet it, or to realize that it doesn't really exist," says McDermott.

Judaism on the other hand believes we have only one life to live, and we'd better concern ourselves with the flesh and blood of the here and now while understanding our relationship to history. "Rhythms and cycles are fundamental to Judaism," declares Irvin Ungar, a "pulpit" rabbi for thirteen years and presently the owner of Historicana Rare Books and Manuscripts in Burlingame, California. He describes the overriding message in Judaism as *tikkun olam*, which literally means to "repair the world," to make it a better place. Ungar says, "All ritual, all ceremony and pomp are to enable us to fulfill this purpose." Another cornerstone of Jewish practice is to make time sacred and meaningful, to make it count. "God blessed time. It is the first thing the Bible considers to be holy," notes Ungar. This is expressed and fulfilled by observing the Sabbath and other holy times and days, making them "unique, different and set aside."

Through regular practices, Judaism aims to fulfill the words of the first-century sage, Hillel, who said, "If I am not for myself, who will be for me? If I am only for myself, what am I? If not now, when?" Ungar adds, "Running through this is the idea of *mitzvah*, a divine or religious obligation that one performs not because it makes us or anyone else feel good. One does it out of acknowledgment that there is something greater than us, that some of us call 'God,' that moves us to do these things."

So central to Judaism are the holidays, Rabbi Irving Greenberg writes in *The Jewish Way: Living the Holidays*, that they are the "quintessential Jewish religious expression . . . the unbroken master code of Judaism. Decipher them and you will discover the inner sanctum of this religion. Grasp them and you hold the heart of the faith in your hand."

Christianity shares many fundamental principles with Judaism, its progenitor: one God (sort of), the Ten Command-ments, and so on. But Christianity's big overriding message is that God loves us so much that He gave His only son, Jesus Christ, who suffered and died a horrible death so that we may have everlasting life. Love is cyclical: God loves us, and Christians believe that our reason for being here is to love God, ourselves and all of our fellow human beings, as God and Jesus love us. It is not enough to say this in our words, or even just feel it in our hearts— although simple faith carries great weight—we must also show this in our actions.

As is the case with Judaism, Christianity poses a tough script to follow, day in and day out. It's human nature to slip up. Its simple doctrine has spawned a complex yearly liturgical calendar of events and holidays. Reverend Robert Cormier, an associate pastor in New Jersey, supplies this insight:

> Cycles are about helping us remember what we believe in,
> giving people a chance to focus on it and talk about it. We
> need to be reminded again and again not because we forget
> the doctrine, but because life chips away at what we have.

In other words, holy days are reminders of what Christians
believe, and reminders also to worship and celebrate those beliefs.
Rituals give people a chance to reapply their faith, re-experience,
and face challenges so they can increase their understanding and
apply it to their own earthly lives. "You become more sharp with
your faith, and it becomes clearer to you," Cormier believes.

For Reverend Sharon Blackburn, the minister of the
Plymouth Church of the Pilgrims, repetition is in part a learning experience. "We need to keep repeating the liturgy of the
yearly church cycle because there is so much to learn. Pastors
conduct the services over and over again throughout their lifetimes and continue to discover new understandings and nuances.
It's impossible for it to grow stale, to exhaust its meaning."

Islam, which grew out of both Judaism and Christianity,
shares their core belief in one Supreme Being. The name Islam
is derived from a word meaning "peace" but also which means
"surrender." This is the attribute Islam most seeks to cultivate—
total surrender to God, to Allah. With this surrender comes
obedience to Allah, which expresses itself in the Five Pillars of
Islam. Islam's rhythms and cycles include praying five times a
day in Arabic, one pilgrimage to Mecca during one's lifetime,
routine charity to the poor, fasting once a year and frequent repetition of the *shahadah* (a reminder that there is no God but
Allah and that Mohammad is his prophet). Devoted Muslims are
therefore highly disciplined and responsible, and rituals and
practices form the framework for this way of being in the world.

Sufism, which is usually described as a mystical sect of Islam, began as a less rigid discipline. Sufism seeks to *feel* God's presence through ecstasy achieved in part through repetitive hypnotic music and dance called *sama*, such as that performed by the immensely popular whirling dervishes.

TO HONOR, TO REMEMBER

Lofty as these purposes are, religious practices didn't materialize out of thin air. They are many-layered and their origins bestow other meanings that make for rich traditions. Rituals mark historical events (escape from Egypt, the birth of Jesus, the pilgrimage to Mecca); personal lifetime events (birth, coming of age, marriage, death); and natural events (seasons, harvest, sunrise and sunset, a full or new moon). That's why, when we observe them, they help us remember and learn from history, make the big and little transitions of our own life cycles and they help to make us conscious of the pulses of nature. By marking historic milestones as a way to celebrate and remember important events in the lives of holy persons, a religion and its people, history is not just memories of past events—but rather full of meaning and vitality for the present.

In Judaism, human history "is the arena of God's purposeful activity," writes Huston Smith. The Jewish people believe that God shapes history so that we can learn from it. That's why history has such great meaning, and is at the forefront of the Jewish holidays. Why would God have imposed such suffering on the Jews, if not for the purpose of helping them learn how to be better people? To help Jews remember history, important days are ordained in the Torah to be celebrated at set times. According to Leviticus, for example, "In the fourteenth day of the first month at even is the Lord's Passover."

Passover, the most holy time in the Jewish year, celebrates

the delivery of Israel from hundreds of years of Egyptian slavery, an event the Jewish people vow to never forget. Leviticus also says, "Six days shall work be done: but the seventh day is the Sabbath of rest," and the Jewish Sabbath commemorates that seminal historic event, the creation of all life. There are also modern commemorative holidays added by the state of Israel, including Holocaust Remembrance Day and Israel Independence Day, which mark monumental changes in the situation of the Jewish people in the world. Judaism emphasizes historic events so that they are not forgotten and because, as Albert Vorspan says in his conclusion to *The Jewish Home* by Damiel B. Syme, "Only a Jewish life which is knowledgeable and rooted in Jewish history and practice can truly be authentic."

Knowing about the history of one's people can be a huge part of a person's identity, and for the Jewish people, who nearly disappeared so many times, knowledge of their history and of Judaism is a core value. Leslie Koppelman Ross, a rabbi and author of *Celebrate!: The Complete Jewish Holidays Handbook* writes, "Each holiday presents its own history lesson," and this in turn offers "a moral message, and opportunity for growth." She continues: "Throughout the long exile, holidays provided relief from a dark existence and reinforced a belief in a better life. . . . Through the rhythm of the Jewish year, our grandparents and great-grandparents and their forebears learned to live as Jews. We see what happened to us, how we are supposed to behave and the long-term reasons behind our actions."

In Christianity, there are two "grand yearly cycles" and they are based on the major events not of an entire people, but of the life of a single person: Christ. Christmas celebrates his birth, and the four weeks of Advent, which come before it, are the preparation for this momentous event. Frank Tedeschi, managing editor at the Church Publishing Company, calls this "the coming cycle." The other major event is Easter, a celebration of the resurrection of Christ, and the six weeks of Lent that come before it; this is "the death-resurrection cycle." In fact, the entire church year is organized around these events, which the liturgy aims to present as a unified picture of the events leading up to Christ's redemption. But these events are more than just an organizing principle that gives structure to the church year.

For Pastor Cormier, celebrating the life of Jesus "is a concrete way of seeing that God is love, and wants us to give of ourselves, the way God gave of himself in his son." Tedeschi reminds us that "Christianity is also about the second coming of Christ and the end of this life and the beginning of life that is unknown and indescribable. All Christians should be living in the tension of knowing that this present age is an incomplete and passing one. It is to be completed by the return of Christ." So, while Christians wait, they celebrate, commemorate and reenact events of the life of Christ.

The Buddhist religious year varies according to the culture, but all holidays revolve around the life of Buddha, or Siddhartha, its founder. Buddhists celebrate three major events: Buddha's birth, his Enlightenment and his death or final Nirvana. In some countries, these milestones are efficiently celebrated all on the same day. To this may be added other historical events such as the death anniversaries of prominent figures in that culture's Buddhist history.

In Hinduism, the history of the gods—and there are hundreds of them—figure predominantly in their yearly calendar. There are many stories of the gods' origins, feats and mischief—and Hindus love to commemorate them with holidays. Each deity embodies some aspect of Brahman—the ultimate reality—much like the Christian saints represent some aspect of the Divine, and may graciously intervene in certain areas, such as travel, money or the welfare of children.

ECHOES OF REMEMBRANCE

Nature worship was probably the first religion. Before clocks and calendars and electronic organizers, before virtual church services, Jewish High Holy Day Websites and Muslim prayer times posted on the Internet, before the Bible, the Talmud or the Qur'an were written, even before sundials measured time, humans were in awe of the powerful rhythms of nature. We hoped the sun would rise again, cold and ice would yield to warmth, rain would fall, plants would grow and babies would be born, that the gift of life would be given again.

Thus, we invented magic and rituals, sacred chants and songs and dances in an effort to make this so. We paid tribute to and worshiped the sun, moon, trees and rivers. We sacrificed animals and firstborns to placate the spirits. We staged huge festivals to celebrate a fertile earth and a bountiful harvest. Spring festivals burst forth with gladness at the rebirth of the earth after a long, cold and dark winter. The spring and autumnal equinox, when day and night are of the same length, were recognized as the special moments they are. Even today, the timing of almost all holidays in all religions—including the universally celebrated New Year—is determined by the position of the sun, moon or other natural bodies.

Most people don't realize (and some just don't care to admit) that pagan rites are the forebears of many practices such as chanting and lighting candles. Many of the most beloved Jewish commemorative holidays are actually transformed agricultural festivals. For example, Passover, which commemorates the liberation from Egyptian slavery, was originally a spring festival. Shavuot, which commemorates the revelation of the Torah to Moses on Mt. Sinai, was in earlier times an elaborate celebration of the grain harvest. As author and theologian Abraham Heschel has noted, these holidays still resonate with the ancestral days that inspired them, even though to Israel, the rhythms and gifts of nature were less significant than the historic events they became associated with.

Christianity has sought to bury its nature-loving pagan influences too. But it's no accident that the resurrection-oriented Easter comes every spring, a time of seasonal rebirth (at least in the Northern Hemisphere, where it originated). And Ember Days, which observe the seasons and the gifts of God's bounty, are among the most ancient Christian observances. Although these are barely noticed today, "ember" is derived from a Latin expression meaning "of the four times or seasons." Today, they survive as the official times of ordination. Rogation Days, three days of special prayer and fasting, are also on few Christian's to-do lists, but were extremely important in an earlier, agrarian society. Yet, both are on the Christian calendar, and the Book of Common Prayer suggests a Rogation Days' prayer that God's "gracious providence may give and preserve to our use the harvests of the land and of the seas."

Today our religions sound faint echoes of these earth-spirit times. This type of ritualistic nature appreciation survives more strongly in many of the existing "primal" religions of the world, particularly those of the polytheistic persuasion and those flourishing in primarily agrarian regions. According to R.S. Ellwood, in his book *Alternate Altars*, much of the recent attraction to pagan religions (and Zen) is due to the attention they pay to the sacred rhythms and ecology of the planet that the Judeo-Christian tradition has "too much slighted."

In countries and regions where most people live a life tied to the land, holidays and rituals sanctify the annual changes of the seasons and the production of food that is so intimately connected with them. For example, in parts of India observing a solar calendar, the festival of Ponkal combines sun worship with ancestor and cattle worship, and with a ritual cooking of the new rice. Everywhere, religious activity intensifies around the summer solstice, a time that corresponds with the beginning of the monsoon season, which is tied to a successful rice crop. The monsoon season shapes religious life in Buddhist Southeast Asia as well. Buddha's birthday is widely celebrated at the beginning of the rains; the end of planting season is celebrated and the rice harvest coincides with another Buddha-related holiday.

The life cycle of an individual is another age-old impetus for religious ritual. It may take a village to raise a child, but it also takes a village to see him or her through the rest of a spiritual life. Although individual customs vary, the points at which divine blessings and covenants are needed vary remarkably little through the ages and among spiritual traditions. Naming ceremonies, initiations, maturity, couplings, childbirth and parenthood, death—these milestones are universally recognized and celebrated with joy, solemnity or sadness.

Our deep-seated need to pay attention to these universal human experiences has been obvious to anthropologists for decades. They realized that the rites of passage in the societies they studied were developed to "carry people across difficult thresholds of transformation," write Kathleen Wall and Gary Ferguson in *Rites of Passage*. "Rituals were not the incomprehensible mumbo jumbo of childlike and superstitious people but deeply rooted and meaningful signposts that pointed the way to human growth and change."

Even lapsed believers or nonbelievers find comfort in traditional religious rituals. Starhawk, a self-proclaimed witch of Jewish descent, lost her mother, a psychotherapist who had rebelled against the orthodoxy of her parents, several years ago. Yet, as her mother lay dying, Starhawk asked her if she wanted to say the *Shemah* with her, a traditional prayer the dying recite, and that is believed to convey the core truth of Judaism. Her mother said yes, and together they repeated the words. Starhawk writes in *The Pagan Book of Living and Dying*, "As we recited the words together, I felt a profound sense of grief. Here was a prayer that, as a child, I had said every night before I went to sleep, the prayer was on the lips of martyrs as they died, the prayer that the victims of the Holocaust remembered as they went to the gas chambers. The prayer said by all my ancestors back for thousands of years. In saying it together with mother as she died, I felt connected to all of them."

THE SCIENCE OF SACRED RHYTHMS

So, rituals and regular worship are good for our spiritual lives. This chapter could end right here. But isn't it interesting that rhythms and cycles are one area where religion and science are growing ever closer? Scientists are coming up with hard evidence for what the ancients discerned by observation or divine transference: that there is an order to the universe, and a tempo to time that is both mysterious and logical. Popular writers are writing best-selling books (*The Tao of Physics* and *The Dancing Wu Li Masters*, to name two of the earliest and most notable) that explain the remarkable parallels between East Asian philosophies—Hinduism, Buddhism, Taoism—and modern physics.

Many scientific studies are related to the recent rediscovery that the mind and body are connected to each other. Our mental state affects our physical state, and vice-versa. Since spiritual concerns are part of the intellectual life of the mind, it would follow that spirituality affects physical health. In fact, many recent studies show that faith and religious activities such as prayer and worship attendance can be helpful in preventing or treating illness, recovering from surgery, reducing pain and improving quality of life. Religious practices offer a meaningful way to tap into this basic connection and give our physical and mental health a boost.

For example, two recent headline-making longevity studies found that people who attend religious services once or more a week live around eight years longer than those who do not. Other studies have shown that religious faith contributes to recovery from depression and is important in preventing it in the first place. In a study of elderly men, the subjects said that going to church helped them cope with illness and enhanced their social life and relationships. In another study of seniors, religious involvement was associated with less physical disability as well as less depression. Other studies show: death rates are lower than expected before important holidays, suggesting that faith and the desire to take part in a tradition may postpone death; churchgoers have nearly half the risk of heart attack and lower blood pressure than non-churchgoers; and patients undergoing open-heart surgery who were religious were three times more likely to survive. Clearly, something is going on here. A resercher for one of the longevity studies concludes:

> There is still a sense among much of the scientific community that religious effects are minor at best or even irrelevant. Our findings help to dispel such a notion.

For some, the idea that God works in mysterious ways is enough of an explanation. Scientists, however, yearn to know the physical mechanism underlying such effects. Some of the effects are surely due to the fact that religious belief is associated with less likelihood of health-destructive behaviors such as smoking and alcohol abuse and sexual promiscuity, while encouraging strong social bonds—all factors that can improve health. But in addition, some spiritual practices can have measurable effects on the metabolism.

Dr. Herbert Benson, a cardiologist and director of the Mind-Body Medical Institute at Beth Israel Deaconess Medical Center in Boston, is a pioneer in this work. He has shown that the repetitive prayer found in most faiths—Jewish davening, reciting the Roman Catholic rosary, Zen meditation—induces a quiet state known as the "relaxation response" and can lower heart and respiration rates and slow brain waves. In dozens of highly regarded experiments, Benson's subjects generated significant reductions in heart attacks and infertility, controlled arthritic pain, PMS and many other ailments, and showed improved mood and memory. Their medical bills were thirty-six percent lower than those who did not pray.

The results of these and other mind-body experiments are so remarkable that scientists have developed a new field of study, called *psychoneuroimmunology*, which seeks to explain such effects through the connection between the emotions, nervous system and hormonal system. However, there must be more to prayer than biochemistry, something beyond jazzed up hormone molecules boosting the immune system. How to explain the finding that heart patients who were prayed for by their loved ones had a higher cure rate—even though they didn't know they were being prayed for?

Another example of science supporting age-old religious practices is the field of chronobiology, which studies circadian (daily) and other biological rhythms. Recent findings support much of the theory behind many practices of Ayurveda, the 4,000-plus-year-old health system that is an integral component of Hinduism. According to Ayurveda, each 24-hour day consists of four-hour segments, each with its own vibrational characteristics which we need to consider in our daily routines such as waking, sleeping, praying, chanting, bathing, eating, exercising and mental tasks. If the characteristics of our actions are not in sync with the characteristics of the hour of the day, we are in effect throwing sand in the gears of our biochemical clocks, causing imbalance and ill health.

Ayurveda was ahead of its time. Chronobiology has discovered that humans (and other animals) do indeed have biological clocks and that these are sensitive to oscillating environmental cues that result from the earth's movements. Our biology has daily, weekly, monthly and even yearly cycles. Our biological processes wax and wane, peak and dip over predictable schedules. Body temperature, digestion, blood pressure, hormone production—all depend on a daily or other cycle. Certain illnesses are more likely to occur at certain times of day—asthma attacks are more frequent between 2 a.m. and 6 a.m.; more heart attacks occur in the morning.

These body rhythms in turn influence the effectiveness and toxicity of drug therapy and surgery, with remarkable results when the timing is right, especially in the case of cancer. We are particularly sensitive to light. We are designed to grow drowsy and sleep during most hours of darkness and be awake and alert during most of the daylight hours. If we tinker with our light exposure, fuzzy thinking, jet lag and perhaps even higher risk of certain cancers ensue. A disorder known as SAD—seasonal affective disorder—that affects some people in the light-diminished autumn and winter appears to respond to light therapy.

A strong scientific argument for keeping the Sabbath—or some version of the seventh day of rest—comes from Witold Rybcynski, in his book *Waiting for the Weekend*. He describes the history of the seven-day week and the worldwide rhythm of six days on, one day off. Despite several attempts to tinker with this pattern by, for example, the French Republic and the Soviet Union, "the week has proved remarkably resilient to such official challenges," he writes. This suggests that the seven-day rhythm "might be the result of a physiologic imperative . . . a weekly maintenance break, analogous to the body's requirement for a certain number of regenerative hours of sleep or a given amount of food and water," he writes. Also, science has detected circaseptan (seven-day) rhythms in several functions of the body, including heartbeat, blood pressure and temperature, acid content of the blood, calcium in the urine and cortisal in the adrenal glands. The seven-day weekly rhythm may be an instinctual way of staying in sync with our body's innate calendar.

All of which seems to bring us back to Ecclesiastes' prescription to be mindful that there is a time for everything, and we tamper with the timing at our peril.

A TIME TO MAKE TIME

As Rabbi Ungar says, religious practices have been time-tested, refined and burnished by several millennia of experience; "they can help us find a way to walk through life with a certain grace." Together, they add up to a lifetime of acknowledging God, Allah, the Ultimate Reality, the One or the Divine, and glisten like jewels on the continuum that is the journey of religion through time. Prayer, readings, song, music, gestures, ritual bathing, dance, offerings—these are the ingredients that comprise the faithful's work and celebration. Sound-silence, movement-stillness, light-darkness, feasting-fasting, celebration-mourning, solitude-community, youth-maturity, death-everlasting life—these are the aspects of the divine tension that fuels religion and propels all life with a vitality that can only exist in the energy of such dynamism.

In a time of floundering around, religious practices give us a firm and fertile foundation for both inquiry and strengthening of faith. In a time of isolation and shaky family foundations, they offer connection and unity. In a time of identity crisis, they provide us with a shared history, an identity. As one elderly Jewish gentleman said, "I'm not religious, but I like to keep the traditions." He takes part because it is something that people of his faith have been doing for hundreds of years, because it has been done millions of times before, and he is part of that thread. "It is who I am. It is us."

Religious rituals are worth the effort because in a time of faster, faster, faster, they offer us a means and a reason to take a breath and slow down. In a time of growing ecological peril, they offer us a spiritual connection with nature. In a time of stubborn religious intolerance, they give us a glimpse of common ground. In a time of anything goes, they give us a framework for discipline. But most of all, they allow us to ask important questions of ourselves and of our religion. "The more you try to save time, the more you realize how little you have," says Rabbi Ungar. And, he says:

> There may be time to retool your investment portfolio, but where's the time to repair the world you live in? The more time we spend thinking about how we can move ahead, the less time we have to think about, How as a community, can we move ahead? Time is a gift. It is precious, and only a certain amount has been allocated to us. Rituals like keeping the Sabbath are a way to sit back and reflect on the meaning of time and the meaning of our lives, to ask the fundamental question:
>
> *How do we want to spend our time?*

2. *Sound and Silence*

Rhythm is originally the rhythm of the feet. Every human being walks, and since he walks on two legs with which he strikes the ground in turn and since he only moves if he continues to do this, whether intentionally or not, a rhythmic sound ensues.

—Elias Canetti, *Crowds and Power*

The Ancients sang their way all over the world. They sang the rivers and ranges, salt-pans and sand dunes. . . . Wherever their tracks led they left a trail of music.

—Bruce Chatwin, *The Songliness*

Listen.

Right now, as you read this, thousands of holy men in India are chanting sacred Sanskrit verses and mantras. This chanting has been going on every minute of every day, perhaps for thousands of years. The holy men believe this is very important work: they chant not only to raise their consciousness, but to make sure the earth stays in balance and harmony for their sake and for all of humankind. If they cease, chaos would ensue, and usher in the end of life as we know it.

Listen again.

The Indian monks are not alone. At this very moment, some-where in the world, a Muslim is also reciting the Qur'an in a mel-lifluous voice, a Jew is praying the Kaddish in cadences as old as time, a Christian is making a joyful noise unto the Lord, a Hindu is chanting as she bathes in the sacred waters of the Ganges, a Buddhist is meditating on the sound of one hand clapping. Day after day, week after week, month after month and year after year, in synagogues, temples, churches, chapels, tekkes, zendos, homes and other sacred spaces, the devout and doubters alike shout out loud, whisper softly, clap their hands, play their organs, beat their drums to praise, worship, invoke and feel the spirit. Truly, the sounds we make in the name of our Maker—the rhythmic songs, the cycles of prayers, the recitations and the silences between them—are as infinite in number as the wonders of the universe.

Sound, particularly in the form of music, is often what attracts us most strongly to a house of worship. "It's pretty well agreed that the two main things that compel people to go to church are the music and the preaching, and these are sound based," says Father Cormier, associate pastor of a Roman Catholic parish. Rosa Lamoreaux, a soprano whose repertoire consists almost exclusively of sacred music, says although music is not what drew her to the church originally, it is what kept her there for many years. Even though she no longer attends church regularly, she listens and sings, and thus is bathed almost con-stantly in sacred sound. "I worship through music," she says. And for Latif Bolat, a musician and singer of Turkish devotion-al songs, "My devotional practice is my music."

Sound can shatter glass, so why should we wonder at its abil-ity to move the soul and bring us closer to the greatness of God? Through sound, God communicates with us, and we with God and our fellow human beings. As all religions know, words and music can lift the spirit to the uppermost heavens, or draw it down to the very depths of sorrow. Sound can help us express our innermost emotions of great joy or great sadness. Sound is cathartic, especially when experienced or created communally. Words can heal. Through words we learn and teach. But words also can hurt more than any tangible stick or stone, whether flung by a child or intoned by a preacher. Remember, Joshua used horns and voices to bring down the walls of Jericho.

In a simple story from the Jewish wisdom tradition, all the limbs of the body have a fight as to who is the most important and indispensable. The feet claim they are, because without them, the person couldn't get from place to place. The hands claim they are, because they are needed to execute basic daily tasks. The jaws claim they are because without them, a person can't eat and take in nourishment. And so on. The tongue claims, "I am." All the other organs laugh at the tongue. But then the person utters a treasonous statement and is jailed and put on death row. "Now do you see how powerful I am?" says the tongue. "My words can get all of you killed." The person recanted his statement and was freed, and all the limbs acquiesced to the tongue's point of view.

Whence sound's miraculous powers? This is one of the great ancient mysteries in both the spiritual and scientific realms. Sound, it seems, is a potent form of energy. Silence, far from being empty or the mere absence of sound, is a profound way to "be" with that energy and enhance its effects, while conveying a power and meaning all its own. Sacred sounds form a bridge between the Divine and the human, and thus between the spirit and the material world. In some religions, sounds *are* the Divine. Sound was and is the most fundamental rhythm of all, a rhythmic wave traveling unseen through the air, a dancing arrow that always finds its mark.

THE GENESIS OF SOUND

Our journey into sound starts at the very beginning of time, at the moment of Creation itself. Ancient peoples believed that before the Creation, there was infinite silence. This silence was broken by the utterance of a sacred sound out of which poured all the energy and matter in the universe. Once the universe was created, sound continued to be connected to "sacred planes of existence." Sound was considered to be the earthly reflection of a fundamental cosmic vibration that was near to the heart and meaning of everything.

We find the idea of the universe's creation by a divine being through some sort of vibration lingers to a greater or lesser degree in all religions. (It is also present in astrophysics: what is the Big Bang but a Really Big Sound?) According to David Tame in *The Secret Power of Music*, these universal vibratory energies were called The Word or The Words of the Gods by the ancient Egyptians; the music of the spheres by the ancient Greeks and the celestial energies of perfect harmony by the ancient Chinese. The Sumerians believed the universe was created when the gods issued their "mighty commands." In the myths of the Celts, the Mayans, and the Native Americans the first god or gods created matter and all life through a sacred word or words. Judaism, Christianity and Islam refer to "The Word" as the utterance of God or as God Himself. For example, in the Gospel according to St. John we read, "In the beginning was The Word, and The Word was with God, and The Word was God." Compare this with the Hindu Vedas, which proclaim, "In the beginning was Brahman, with whom was the Word. And the Word is Brahman." One might think this was either coincidence or plagiarism—or Universal Truth.

So, religions agree that sound is seminal. Ancient China took this notion to the nth degree and made sacred sound the basis of an elaborate structure for the entire civilization. There, sound was thought to be the fundamental vibration and music the embodiment of all the elements of the celestial harmony that governed the universe. The ancient text *Li Chi* says, "Music is the harmony of heaven and earth. Through harmony all things are made known."

But not just any old music would do: the ancient Chinese divided the primal sound into twelve cosmic tones, each associated with one of the twelve zodiacal regions of the heavens, and with each astrological month of the year. Whichever tone was the "tone of the month" was more prominent than the others, and all ceremonial music played that month had to be performed in that tone. The twelve tones were believed to maintain harmony in the heavens and on earth—but only if the composition and the performance were up to par. In those days, matter and energy were considered to be one and the same; each note was itself "real, living, and vibrant" and the listener "became the notes" as they sounded their portion of the infinite. Therefore, playing and hearing these "correct" sacred tones brought people more in sync with the cosmos and closer to the Source of all Being.

It also brought them closer to good fortune—and the bigger the sound, the greater the effect. Music was so instrumental in ordering existence that the T'ang Dynasty (A.D. 618–907) kept fourteen court orchestras, one consisting of 1,346 musicians. For the solstices and other important festivals, this dynasty is said to have brought together musicians totaling 10,000 or more. Why? According to Tame, "The energy invoked . . . was believed to exert a far-reaching influence into all the affairs of the nation . . . [and] the greater the sound, as well as the more minds actively involved, the greater the proportion of cosmic energy invoked and radiated forth. Thus a vast outpouring went forth with which the entire land could be invigorated and spiritually enlightened." Certain traditions classified particular rhythms and cycles as appropriate to specific gods and ritual activities. If you have trouble keeping the beat to a cha-cha, listen to this: some traditions, such as Tantric Buddhism, use mathematical beat groups extending into the hundreds because they musically embody cosmological and other religious concepts.

FROM OM TO AMEN TO EINSTEIN

Say OM out loud the way the Hindus do, repeating it slowly, your breath emptying from your body in a round, steady stream, the sound rising through three progressive tones. Two little letters, one syllable, not even a word, really. And yet OM in its elegant simplicity has the power to instill a cosmic feeling of peaceful excitement, even when uttered by a lapsed Lutheran. Could the Hindus be right—is the power of OM due to its role as the vibration of the life-giving energies of the whole universe? Does uttering it actually attune the utterer to the ultimate celestial tone itself?

"The syllable OM, which is the imperishable Brahman, is the universe. Whatsoever has existed, whatsoever exists, whatsoever shall exist hereafter, is OM. And whatsoever transcends past, present, and future, that is also OM." So says the Mandukya Upanishad. Whew! No wonder OM has become a multi-purpose sound used in private and public chants and meditation, a kind of Ur-mantra. And no wonder Jewish and Christian services are punctuated with so many Amens—they are considered to be the cosmic equivalent of OM.

Similar to the ancient Chinese primal sound, Hinduism's OM (sometimes spelled AUM) shapes, originates and sustains physical matter. All that exists is therefore considered to be vibratory—cyclic, wavelike or oscillatory in nature. This is where Einstein meets Brahman. Einstein's theory of relativity states that energy (vibration) and matter (the physical world) are the same. Modern physics has discovered that atoms and subatomic particles are distressingly insubstantial. What we were taught were tiny solar systems with solid particles revolving around a nucleus—building blocks of the universe—are actually manifestations of energy in a state of vibration or oscillation. Some scientists, in fact, consider the atom to be a kind of resonating musical note. As a chemist from John Hopkins University notes, "If we but had the right ears, we could hear these atoms humming and singing." In this sense, the Chinese and Hindu views of reality were not far off the mark. But can humans actually consciously influence the world through sound—mantras, chanting, prayer—as many religions would have us believe?

BECAUSE I SAID SO

Looking back to the Creation stories we find that even after the first utterance that gave rise to existence, words or sounds were needed to shepherd Creation through the next phases. In the Bible it is written:

> And God said, Let there be light: and there was light . . . And God said, Let the waters under the heaven be gathered together unto one place, and let the dry land appear: and it was so . . . And God said, Let the earth bring forth grass, the herb yielding seed, and the fruit-tree after his kind, whose seed is in itself, upon the earth: and it was so.

And so on, through the moon and stars, the fish, and fowl and every animate and inanimate thing. The words themselves seem to spark creation: God speaks each thing and, in describing it and naming it, it manifests. In Egyptian myth we find gods creating themselves and other gods by visualizing them and uttering their names, and then proceeding to use the same process to create the things and beings of the world. Whether you take this literally or allegorically, the point is that some form of sound from a higher dimension is used and these sounds are referred to as words of an earthly language.

The Egyptians also believed that the God Ra gave certain

secret words of power to the earthly priesthood. Why? So that it, too, might use sound to direct the energies of the cosmos to influence conditions on earth. This implies that Genesis is not finished; it is ongoing, in an eternal process of creation and preservation by cosmic sound. Indeed, Hindus see Natural Law as continually unfolding in specific sequential stages. The ancient seers recognized these stages as sounds and set them down in the sacred texts known as Vedas.

These sounds, called *shruti* ("that which is heard"), are sometimes thought of as packets of intelligence. These packets contain the codes—like the DNA in our genes—that structure the creation of the universe, maintain it, dissolve it and reconstitute it in the endless cycle that is life. Thus, everything in the universe—every object and process in creation—has its subtle constituent sound pattern or combination of patterns. If we knew the particular sound of an object and could reproduce it, we would have incredible power over the universe. From here it is just a short hop to mantras, chants, prayers, affirmations and songs—the kit of audible parts that are woven throughout so many religious practices and rituals and that are believed to harness such powers.

Hinduism has perhaps the most elaborate cosmology of sound of any world faith tradition. A devout Hindu's day is filled with prayers, chants, mantras and songs. Like the rest of us, Hindus sing in the shower, but in addition to enhancing the exuberant sensual pleasures of bathing, this has the added significance of enhancing the purification effects of the water. Hinduism has come to see life as one long song because sound can be used to influence everything. David Tame writes in *The Secret Power of Music*, "To the yogi, the OM is as immediate as the air around him, sounding out in the eternal present. It beats the rhythm of all hearts, and speaks to the soul having ears to hear . . . the Creation was not done . . . the morning stars still sing together."

Listen. Listen to your breathing, your mouth watering, your

throat swallowing, your heart beating, your stomach gurgling, your thoughts crashing into one another. It is the sound of you, of creation still in the process of creating, of OM, of Amen, of church bells ringing, of horns blowing, of Indian monks chanting for all time.

PRAYER: SAYING THE UNSAYABLE

If sound was the spark of Creation, how fitting that sound is the ultimate tool to express our thanks for all the blessings that continue to emerge from that divine act. Prayer is the main way we reach our Maker and is the word most often used to describe a seamless spectrum of the sounds of faith. It is the bedrock of religious practices, both private and public, in daily worship and on special occasions. Prayer is an absolute necessity in most religions as a means to bridge the obvious gap between the divine and human worlds. (Except of course in Buddhism, where there is no gap.)

The Hasidic Rebbe Menachem Mendel has come up with this lovely image: "God sends souls down to earth and brings them back by making them all climb ladders." And prayer is the best known, most popular, and most successful "ladder," says Rabbi Wayne Dosick, in *Living Judaism*. "Prayer is the personal journey that brings you to encounter God, the quest that takes you to both the depths and heights of your emotions, the voyage that transcends time and place, and transforms the very essence of your being. Prayer is your shout of joy, your cry of anguish, the ultimate whisper of your heart and soul." Thomas Merton wrote in *The Sign of Jonas*, "Prayer is the potent vehicle for the most intimate union with God." And William James in *Varieties of Religious Experience* writes that "in prayer, spiritual energy, which otherwise would slumber, does become active, and spiritual work of some kind is effected." For Muslims, who join movement with prayer in a practice called *salat*, prayer is a "luminous event" that engages the entire being. It "lends a new life to the day, binding it into the rhythm of a sacred cycle," writes Coleman Barks in *The Illuminated Prayer*. For author Herman Wouk, the daily aim of prayer is "a renewal of religious energy through an act which declares one's Jewish identity and one's hope in the Lord."

But where on earth do prayers come from? In the Jewish tradition, prayers grew out of the need to find a practical substitute for the sacrificial offerings of animals and agricultural products with which Jews originally worshipped God. Destruction of the first and second holy temples combined with exile led the Jewish people to use portable prayers of words for atonement and grace, instead of sacrifices at altars that no longer existed. Early Christians, who were converted Jews, continued the practice, but in their own words. Islam has a more poetic version: Prayer is God's gift to humankind. Angels who prayed in celestial adoration, and then taught it to humans, were the first to practice the daily *salat*.

Whatever their origin, words and sounds are the foundation, the bricks and the mortar of worship services. In the Jewish tradition, the sages developed a fixed order or structure of prayer and this became standardized for each prayer service. The evening, morning and afternoon service was shaped to follow its unique natural rhythms, day in and day out, with monthly and yearly holiday services obeying their own set structures. In Christianity, too, each Sunday, weekday and holiday service has become carefully composed and choreographed to display a certain rhythmic ebb and flow of sounds and silences. There are highs and there are lows. There are moments of breathtaking drama and quiet contemplation, times of individual worship and communal participation.

Each time one attends a worship service, one repeats the familiar prayers, chants and mantras over and over again. Personal prayer may be spontaneous and free, "a pouring out of the heart before God," according to Friedrich Heiler, author of many books on religion. But many times the prayer in one's thoughts or one's lips is a standardized one. For example, in Judaism the Kaddish is recited after reading the Bible or at the close of synagogue prayers; in Christianity the Lord's Prayer is recited during every service and daily during private devotions and in Islam the salat is recited five times a day, every day. When such set prayers are repeated many times, isn't there the danger of them becoming static or done on automatic pilot?

SAY IT AGAIN, SAM

The Jewish sages realized the value of standardization and repetition. They aimed to satisfy a person's need and desire to check in with God at the beginning, middle and end of the day and established a day-in and day-out morning, afternoon and evening prayer practice. Likewise, the first Christians recited the *Our Father* prayer three times a day. Muslims pray five times a day, interweaving their entire day with prayer. Repetition, far from being boring, seems to be desirable where prayer is concerned, and it's not because the unceasing verbal barrage enhances your chance of getting a busy God's attention.

For one thing, repetitive prayer seems to contribute to the continuity and communication of tradition and culture. The formulaic character of liturgical prayers actually makes participation more inviting because it establishes a frame of expectation, a pattern that becomes familiar. According to studies of language and speech, rote ritualistic repetition can move rather than dull the spirit. It can persuade, name, commit, promise, affirm; it can strengthen emotion, sustain courage and excite hope.

Repeated day after day, religious services are designed to bring a spiritual connection and uplift which might otherwise elude worshipers. As writer Lisa Grunwald observes, "Out of repetition, sometimes magic is forced to rise." This could explain why one rarely "feels anything" if one attends worship service

sporadically. It's a vicious cycle: you don't attend services regularly because they are meaningless, and they are meaningless
because you don't go regularly. Even in formula prayer, there is
room for infinite subtle variety and growth—because of changing
conditions, and because *we* change everyday. That's why with
each repetition the meaning becomes clearer and truer—the
words don't change, but we do, and that's partly because of our
exposure to the repetition. There is also sometimes room for per-
sonalization, as is the case in the daily prayer to cure ill people,
one can insert the name of the persons who need healing instead
of just saying the generic prayer. And during the *Shma Koleinu*,
the Jewish "hear our voices" prayer, one can insert whatever one
wants to say as an entreaty, like a musician can insert his or her
own interpolation during the cadenza in a concerto.

Sufis have a distinctive worship gathering called *zikr*, which
means remembrance of the Friend, or Allah. The Friend can
also refer to a "spiritual companion" or spiritual leader such as
the famous Shams al-Din of Tabriz and the great Sufi poet Rumi
were to each other. Participants chant the name of the Friend
and short phrases of praise and worship of Allah for hours at a
time, all in Arabic. The idea is to constantly remember the
Friend's essence in your heart, and thus see the Friend in all living beings. "It's very repetitive," says Latif Bolat, a Turkish-born
musician who has played at many zikrs. "Zikr music is trance
music, and when it is performed well, the trance really happens.
You feel almost like you're flying, and you know that a special
moment is happening." Unfortunately, one doesn't always reach
such heights. But as a beautiful woman, full of grace and swathed
in layers of soft clothing said after such a zikr, "People may not
notice it at the time, but something is happening to them, even
if they are not Muslim, because they are bathed in the sounds of
Allah." Like great art, ritual repetition may work on the sub-
conscious level and take some time to realize its effects.

Mantras are a particularly enchanting form of prayer. *Mantra* is a Sanskrit word meaning "sacred utterance" and all Hindu rituals are accompanied by mantras, which can be a single syllable (such as OM) or an entire hymn. Every Brahman worships the sun twice a day, by reciting a three-line verse called the Gayatri mantra. All rites of passage (*samskaras*) contain mantras, and a mantra can be used to sacralize any ordinary act, such as bathing, and to render it more effective. We may think of mantras as uniquely Eastern, but only the word comes from the East, not the concept. Jews have many mantras, most obviously the blessings said throughout the day: *Baruch Atah Adonai, Elehainu, Meloch Ha'Olam* means, "blessed are you, the eternal, our God, Ruler of the Universe." *Nusachs* are special tonal mantras that are sung seasonally, and the Sabbath services change by the month and have special monthly nusachs.

For Muslims, *La ilaha illa'llah* ("There is no god but God!") has become a mantra and is considered to be the greatest phrase of the Arabic language. In the same category is *Bismillah Ir Rahman Ir Rahim*, which is translated as "In the name of Allah, the compassionate, the merciful." This phrase appears at the beginning of every chapter of the Qur'an but one, and is used by Muslims to sanctify endeavors at their beginning—including speeches and radio broadcasts. It may be the most recited group of words in the history of language and is a familiar and comforting sound to Muslims, a strong and constant link in the chain of Islamic brotherhood and sisterhood.

The Psalms of the Bible are mantras, as are some famous toneless prayers that devout Catholics recite. The rosary is a kind of mantra, and its origin is fascinating. It came into being around a time when most people could not read, and prayers became formulaic so as to be easier to commit to memory. This was also the time of the Bubonic Plague, which many Europeans thought was the beginning of the Last Judgment. One of the formula prayers was the Hail Mary—Mary was viewed as a merciful mediator who would intercede to temper the terrible justice of God. So there developed a devotion originally consisting of 150 "Hail Marys," one for each of the 150 Psalms that the literate recited as part of their regular devotions. Thus the rosary was born, in which, as Newark's Father Robert Cormier observes, "the beads free you from having to keep count so you can focus and be really present" in the prayer.

THE SINGING THAT'S NOT A SONG

Some of the most gorgeous, haunting and spiritual vocalizations in existence, hover somewhere between speech and song. Chanting, a way of reciting sacred writing using musical tones, exists in all religions. This singsong style is the traditional way of vocalizing the Psalms (which were written as songs) and canticles in Roman and Anglican churches. And certain charismatic evangelical preachers come close to chanting when they sermonize. The Qur'an is chanted, and so are the Hindu Vedas and Buddhist Scriptures. Scores of Native American medicine people chant daily. In the Jewish tradition a cantor (a trained and talented singer), a bar mitzvah boy or anyone with training can chant the Bible, blessings and certain prayers during the worship service, and lead the congregation in its vocal parts.

Chants may sound alike to the inexperienced ear; but nothing could be further from the truth, although the musicality can be subtle. Chanting implies a free rhythm, a limited range of pitch and a relatively simple melodic style. Chants are usually unaccompanied and, to varying degrees, improvised. Chants may contain "nonsense syllables" to enhance the expression of passionate emotion, as when it takes the Gregorian chanter ten minutes to come to closure on the word "Amen." Or the words may be paramount, with no ornamentation permitted, as in Orthodox Islam.

Hasidic singing is a focal point of the religious experience for this mystical Jewish sect. When they sing, conventional beauty of intonation is not a major concern; rather, the singing reflects a tension of feeling and the yearning for an inner experience of God. A single word may inspire an extended tune, or the melody may incorporate meaningless syllables because this is the best way to express before God feelings that are too intimate or delicate to be expressed in conventional sounds and words. This kind of soul music became coupled with mystical exercises such as intense concentration, fasting and rhythmic body movements.

Certain types of chants are so awesomely beautiful and powerful that they have broken out of the temple, synagogue, church and mosque to be appreciated by a secular, international audience. Today, you can hear chants and other forms of sacred music in concert and buy them, such as Duke Ellington's Sacred Concerts, on CDs. An album based on Gregorian chants has even become a bestseller. Gregorian chant, the traditional music of the Roman Catholic Church, is rooted in pre-Christian Jewish tradition and reached the height of complexity and sophistication in the late Middle Ages in Europe. Another chant form that has achieved worldwide appreciation and acclaim is the Tibetan Buddhist chant called *dbyan*. These chants are very slow, low-pitched—almost a moan. In hearing them, you go back, way back in time, and can hear the vibration of the universe; no wonder they are said to be the most beautiful works in Tibetan music.

Chanting is like a meditation that concentrates all of the singer and listener's attention in the moment. The musical devices such as overtones, toning and repetition can alter your mental, emotional and spiritual state. Steve Halpern, writing in *Sound Health*, points out that chanting is done in monasteries, even where silence and abstinence are obligatory, so the life force of renunciates isn't destroyed by lack of vocal exercise. He further states that singing is related to the sexual and creative channels of

physical life—monks and nuns need to sing to release these energies. As they say in Latin, *Si non copulatus, cantito.*

INSTRUMENTS OF THE BODY AND THE SPIRIT

Sound vibrations have a profound effect on us, whether they are
internal or external, made by the human voice or musical instruments, and whether we are aware of them or not. One effect of
religious music can only be described as soul stirring: you hear
it, and like a baby in your womb, something moves inside you.
What makes music soulful? Is it the melody, the scale, the tone,
the rhythm? The volume? The words? Is it the singer, or the
song? Does it depend on your culture, your background, or your
taste? Since Aretha Franklin could stir some souls by singing the
yellow pages, but even more so by singing "Wholly Holy," and
some souls would remain hard as stone no matter what she sang,
the answer to all these questions must be "yes."

Latif Bolat, singer of Turkish devotional music, is also a music
therapist. He says, "Musical scales have different properties and
different effects because of their intervals and the frequencies
that they produce. It's not just a psychological thing—the different sound waves of different types of music and instruments can
create different effects." The devotional songs he sings are
shaped by centuries-old Sufi poetry. Like gospel music, the music
itself is quite simple and repetitive, with simple melodies that
anyone can follow. But the lyrics are suffused with devotion and
a great longing. And when you add the mesmerizing rise and fall
of rhythms the simple music becomes incredibly complex and
sophisticated. Sacred words set to sacred music deliver a one-two
punch, as Saint Augustine noticed when he wrote, "When these
words of the songs are sung, the sacred words stir my mind to
greater religious fever and kindle in me a more ardent flame of
piety than they would if they were not sung."

The reality of music's physical and psychological effects has been used to advantage not only in purely religious settings. Music therapy has a long history in many traditions, including that of the ancient Chinese, Persians, Egyptians and Greeks. The Arabs of the thirteenth century had music rooms in their hospitals. India has a remarkable repertoire of sacred *ragas*, able to evoke intense spiritual feelings. Some ragas are composed to be in synchrony with the characteristics of the time of day and hence the cosmic vibration, and are used to heal physical, mental and spiritual ills by bringing the person in sync with the cosmos. The Hebrews recorded several instances of musical treatment of emotional and spiritual ailments, the most well known being King David, singer of Psalms, playing a harp to help soothe fellow King Saul's melancholia.

Modern science continues to investigate music's healing properties. Science uses muscle testing, biofeedback, electro-acupuncture and other measurements to show that the entire body responds to sound. All our cells can vibrate and be receptors for sound. Our bodies are actually "living bio-oscillators" that pick up vibrations from radios, cell phones, even garage door openers, writes Steve Halpern. Researchers are discovering that certain kinds of music and sounds can contribute to stress, tension, headache, nausea, hearing loss, disturbed sleep and poor digestion. On the other hand, music can help alleviate depression, anxiety, insomnia, high blood pressure, headaches and asthma.

Listening to spiritual music is one thing, but when we actively create music, we hitch a ride on the pure energy of the universe and become part of the never-ending cycle of creation itself. This is particularly true if the musical instrument is your own voice. Singing allows you to realize your spiritual awareness and to voice your deepest emotions, emotions that words alone can't express. Sacred or spiritual gatherings provide the few opportu-

nities the average person has to sing, and to be an active participant, rather than a passive listener.

The uttered or sung word is more powerful than the written
word because the human voice is the original and most potent
instrument of all—it is intimately physically connected with the
mind and can express most deeply and soulfully the spectrum of the
infinite shades of meaning and spiritual feeling within the singer
and the composer. It is the difference between reading a music score
of Bach's Mass in B minor—and singing it yourself or hearing it
sung by a deeply spiritual, highly trained and talented artist.

Bolat says his singing is really about devotion to the Beloved,
and it gives him a feeling of being a part of a greater picture. He
says that the goal of the Sufi practitioner is to deliver both himself and the listener to an ecstatic, trance state. When he sings,
he often does become "ecstatic." Soprano Rosa Lamoreaux
notices two unique types of experience when she sings:

> When I'm performing, the audience makes me focus more
> deeply, and something happens that doesn't happen to me
> when I am just rehearsing. It's not work anymore, you feel
> the inspiration of the music first and then it comes through
> you, it's almost its own cycle. You're hearing it *and* you are
> creating it. It's humbling. It also seems that if we communi-
> cate and share our innermost being—our soul—when per-
> forming, then we allow ourselves and our listeners to create
> a spiritual atmosphere.

Spiritual music, even mediocre spiritual music, can create a
space and a time that feels sacred, a tangible energy shift that
sets apart from the mundane world outside. Music can bend,
extend and compress time through the tools of cyclicity, repetition, contrast and pattern.

There's something else going on, too. "The process of singing one note for an extended time brings about a number of chemical changes and metabolic processes in the body, including the possible release of endorphins (so-called 'feel-good' chemicals) in the brain, as well as a mental concentration that allows the hemispheres to synchronize their functioning," according to Steven Halpern, author of *Sound Health*. He also points out that singing emphasizes vowel sounds (talking emphasizes consonants), and the three so-called "pure" vowel sounds appear in similar spiritual and healing contexts throughout the world. The "ah" sound appears in Sanskrit as the Aum mantra, in the Adonai of Hebrew, the Allah of Islam and in the Amen and Alleluia of the Judeo-Christian worship. "The pure vowel sounds vibrate with frequencies traditionally associated with particular attributes, energies and parts of the body that resonate to the sound," he continues. Then there is the "M" sound—the words OM, and Amen share this humming characteristic, which vibrates internally.

Let us not forget that many sacred texts—the very foundations of the major religions are words—were spoken, chanted and sung before they were written. The Vedas, the Bible, the Qur'an—these existed first only as sound vibrations, the word of God given to the prophets, oral traditions passed down from generation to generation until they were written down. This explains why they are poetic, often rhyming, and can be repetitious—all devices to aid the reciter's memory and the listener's comprehension. These texts today are still read and recited, and sometimes sung.

Which is not to say that musical instruments are impotent. Drums, bells, organs, stringed instruments, flutes and horns add their own voices, help keep the rhythm and enhance the effect of the human voice or stand on their own. Tibetan bells speak volumes without words at all. The shofar is one of the oldest musical instruments in human history that is still in use. This curved instrument is traditionally made from a ram's horn; prebiblical use focused on its magical ability to blast away evil demons, but in the modern Jewish tradition when it is sounded repeatedly throughout the Rosh Hashanah service it has many meanings. On one level, it is a cry for mercy and forgiveness and recollects the lamentations of all Jewish martyrs. For Maimonides, the great Jewish medieval philosopher and Tamudist, it functions as a wake up call that rouses sleepers to "examine your deeds, return in repentance, and remember your Creator." Rabbi Leon Klenicki says, "It announces and proclaims our messianic hope, in the coming of the day of the Kingdom of God, which we have been told as children. It has immense power—the sound is so deep, we are filled with awe." Herman Wouk describes the experience this way: "The first shrieking blast of the ram's horn in the crowded synagogue chills the spine. The repeated blasts, the weird alterations from long to short, from wailing to straight, shake the nerves. The voice of alarm has not altered in thousands of years. The ram's horn and the air raid siren describe the same sound patterns and do the same thing to the human heart."

According to Reverend Kobutsu Malone, a Zen Buddhist priest, Zen specializes in percussion instruments. He describes the sound of the *han*, a board suspended at the door of the *zendo* (training hall). "It is struck several times a day, in a specific pattern that is done in such as way that it communicates that time, which flies like an arrow, is of the essence. We shouldn't waste it, we should pay attention to what is happening in the present." A picture may be worth a thousand words, but sometimes a wordless sound can say as much or more.

THE MODERNS

So far we have been dealing with ancient and traditional music. What about music composed more recently—gospel, spirituals, jazz, rock and contemporary classical—that we hear with increasing frequency in certain places of worship? This may be an area as contentious as religious doctrine itself.

What some traditions and some individuals praise as spiritual, others condemn as diabolical. What some find incredibly moving leaves others scratching their heads in puzzlement. This has been going on quite some time. In the Middle Ages, innovations and changes to plain chanting (Gregorian chant) by adding instrumental accompaniment were met with horror. In the Renaissance, composers who based their Mass settings on popular folk tunes of the secular world did so at their own peril. When Martin Luther brought in the idea of singing in the vernacular as well as reading the Bible, it divided the Christian Church in half. Innovation and change are part of a continuum—there are always moments of controversy when efforts are made to make music or text more accessible to the average person rather than just some rarefied priestly caste. Or when composers seek to create music of their own, rather than repeat the past.

There are several underlying questions here. For example, where does music come from? How forward looking or backward looking is a religion as expressed in its music?

Some say all the music ever written has been "channeled" from God or the cosmic consciousness. Indeed, J.S. Bach and many other classical composers of sacred music acknowledge divine inspiration: Mozart, for example, said, "I prayed to God and the symphony began." Handel, on his ecstatic experience while writing the Messiah, said, "I did think I did see all heaven before me—and the great God himself. Whether I was in my body or out of my body as I wrote it, I know not, God knows." Wagner believed that "the art of music proceeds from God and dwells in the hearts of all enlightened men." For Hildegard von Bingen, a twelfth-century German nun, music was divine inspiration as well as the highest form of human activity, a mirror of the ineffable sounds of the heavenly spheres and the angels. Her ethereal crystalline spiral harmonies reach profound heights of intensity, sweetness and intimacy; they wail tragically even as they glow with joy and transcendence and otherworldly beauty that is a supreme example of how spirit becomes material and the material spirit.

Is some music channeled from the devil and therefore evil? Or is some music merely banal? Orthodox Islam bans all music from the mosque because rather than being a tool to get closer to God, they believe it is a distraction. In her book *Rumi: A Spiritual Biography*, author Leslie Wines describes how the topic of music has generated much controversy for Sufism, and Islam in general, "largely because instrumental music was not a common or [considered a] sophisticated art form in Arabia during the lifetime of Muhammad. Because there were no indications that Muhammad ever enjoyed musical performances, his spiritual descendants who liked music felt compelled to codify, and justify in extremely precise religious terms, how it could be enjoyed." But according to a Buddhist author, Sa-skya Pandita, all music is praiseworthy because it relieves human suffering.

Lamoreaux makes this distinction: "There's a difference for me, between the sacred, the spiritual and the emotional. There's a depth to classical music—it takes you to a much deeper level of appreciation. It may be a combination of the intellectual and the spiritual, and not purely emotional. Bach, Mozart, Haydn carry a more emotional response; Hildegard von Bingen is hypnotic, the most spiritual music I do. For me, gospel music and spirituals are a different realm, but they can be very heartfelt if done with truth and feeling."

Peter Stoltzfus includes contemporary music in his services, even though for some listeners, it's a stretch. He cites historic precedent for this. "Historically, say in the 1700's, the music used in church worship was all composed in its own day. This is one reason that rock music, for example, in Christian worship, is so exciting—it has a fresh, contemporary feel to it." Furthermore, he points out, the older a culture becomes, the greater the opportunity to draw on all of its past. "The further we go forward in time, the larger the repertoire of artistic responses to the Christian faith. We have at our disposal so much material, that the mood of the worship service can be tailored according to when the music was written."

THE SOUND OF SILENCE

Prayer and music are doubtless wonderful things. One could go on and on about them in their infinite variety. But there would be no sound without silence, just as we would not recognize light without darkness. What can one say about silence? Silence is silence, right? Yes and no. Think about all the places that silence can occur. We can be alone with our silence, during prayer, meditation and contemplation. We can be silent together with other worshippers. We can be silent inwardly or outwardly, or both. There is silence between words and between musical notes, between groups of words and pieces of music, giving them shape.

Silence is an essential element in all religions. Buddhism, and Zen Buddhism in particular, is most strongly associated with silence. Silence is an integral part of meditation, the practice that is at the heart of Zen. Reverend Kobutsu enlightens us: "In Zen, silence is more than just the absence of noise. From the Zen perspective it means not only silence outside your body, but silence inside also. Silence from verbal thought forms, silence from feelings and emotions." In Hinduism, another meditation tradition, silence is esteemed as the mother of sound—sound is created from the apparent muteness of silence. "It is from the silent void, the cosmic 'no-thing-ness' of unbounded consciousness, that all creation comes," writes Alistair Shearer in *The Hindu Vision*.

Although there is much silence in Hindu rituals, there is much sound, too, because the Hindus paradoxically use the senses to go beyond the senses, and nowhere is this more evident than in the use of sound. Chanting the many names of God has a purifying effect on both the nervous system and the atmosphere, Hindus believe. There are few religious rituals more pleasantly and chaotically noisy than the services conducted in a Hindu temple. Attending Sunday morning services at the Hindu Temple Society in Queens is like stepping into a lively bazaar— the sounds of praying and chanting and musical instruments and children playing all competing with each other, the continual swirling movement, the brightly colored saris, flowers, deities and foods. Yet used correctly, Shearer writes, such an abundance of sounds and stimulation can paradoxically "unfurl the finest petals of feeling and transport the mind to that silence which is the mother of all sounds."

Of course there is also a huge tradition of silence in Christianity. The Quaker tradition is one of silence. Christian monks and nuns often take vows of silence. As is to be expected, Thomas Merton, the Trappist who has written extensively about his experiences, is an eloquent advocate of silence. Early in his stay at a Tennessee monastery, he tells God that he is "longing for the holiness of your deep silence." After time he finds even the monastery to be too raucous and writes in his journal, "The High Mass was quite beautiful—first the organ went dead, and that made the sanctuary . . . utterly beautiful." And early on he realizes that "Everything I came here to find seems to me to be concentrated in the twenty or thirty minutes of silent and happy absorption that follow communion when I get a chance to make a thanks giving . . . I like to remain alone and quiet after mass. Then my mind is relaxed and my imagination is quiet and my will drowns in the attraction of a love beyond understanding, beyond definite ideas."

For those of us who are neither monks nor nuns, a church, temple or other house of worship may be one of the few quiet places in which we can take refuge from the din in urbanized areas. And through religious ritual, we can find mystical or divine silence, an indescribable blissful state common to all religions.

Silence is an indispensable element in music. As a musician Rosa Lamoreaux has noticed that "within the music itself there are rests, and those rests are as important as the sounds you are making around those silences. Sometimes they are a moment of release, sometimes a moment of anticipation of what's coming. Silences are alive—they are not passive—but they need to be observed. Spaces between songs are important too, to give the listener time to absorb the song, for the performer to complete that thought. A sacred performance has to do with drama and contrast. Breathers make it more interesting and give it contrasts. As in conversation, you need to pause."

At Plymouth Church of the Pilgrims, Reverend Sharon Blackburn and minister of music Peter Stoltzfus create worship services together. The service is a carefully composed performance of sound and silence in which the congregation observes and takes an active part. Blackburn laments, "In our tradition, we have little opportunity for silence," which is a shame she says because "silence is our opportunity for personal transition. Silence is full and pregnant, it's time to be with God, time to process what has just transpired in the service."

Stoltzfus says, "In the worship service words, music and silence play off each other and amplify each other. After a particularly cogent prayer, admonition or teaching, you are given a moment to reflect and apply it to your own life. In my experience, if a pause is well placed and well timed, it can bring you into a striking awareness of yourself." In this era, when freedom and unlimited options are king, "our everyday life is chaos. Even in church meetings, everyone speaks at once. No one listens. The worship service is ordered in such a way that there is a time to speak, to sing, a time to be silent and listen," Blackburn says. She feels that paradoxically, there is a gorgeous freedom and opportunity in this tidy ordering of events. There is ease and relaxation in knowing what will happen next. The structure may seem closed, but it is really a means of opening up—you are forced to change for an hour each week, to adopt a different way of being. "We're putting ourselves out on the table in a different way. We are allowing ourselves to be far more open in the interchange to the experience of God."

Lamoreaux finds that people are "terribly over-stimulated today." We live in a frenetic world, she says, where people never sit still and the music reflects that.

> I don't listen to music when I run, and I do what you might call a meditation in utter silence. We need quietness and quiet music to give us time to reflect. I can feel the blood pressure drop in a room when I sing Hildegard. I think this is why chant and New Age music have become so popular—people need it to slow down.

In Judaism, just as there is a time for chanting, singing and praying out loud, so too is there a time for silence. For example, Rabbi Klenicki explains, "When we silently recite the eighteen benedictions of the Amidah, that moment of silence is very important because you are by yourself." "Silence," Rabbi Bronstein at B'nai Jeshurun in New York, says, "is the place where the soul unfolds, the moment of peace when the soul can really speak. Without silence, the soul cannot look in the mirror." Some people shun silence because, according to Rabbi Klenicki "it can be dangerous—noise covers the holes in your life." To be sure, it can be overwhelming to suddenly face oneself in the silence, the void, which threatens to suck us in like a vacuum. Klenicki bemoans the lack of quiet in everyday life, and even in the synagogue, where "silence is a luxury—everybody talks, the children are running around. I tell my students to try to recover silence in the New York subway—if you can do that, you have reached a great moment in your life. And then you may be able to recover silence in a noisy synagogue, too."

Sages have long maintained that silence is required for attaining wisdom. In the vision quest of the Algonquins, the young seeker of direction and meaning would go off to fast in solitude and silence. Only by entering the silence would he hear the spirit speaking to him. Silence is believed to be the sign of a wise person, hence the maxim: "He who speaks, does not know; he who knows, does not speak." As the founder of the ecstatic school of Sufism said, "No lamp seen brighter than silence, no speech heard better than speechlessness."

These are wise words indeed. Today, we are surrounded by sound, and little of it is sacred. We are bombarded with the heavy beat of boom boxes, the vapid mood manipulation of Musak, the chatter of TV, the ubiquitous cell phone conveying crucial information such as our friend's current coordinates. If music patterns affect life patterns and the spirit, we would be wise to choose our music and our sounds carefully, to treat music with greater respect, to balance our worldly acoustic realm with sacred sounds and blissful silence. To really listen with our hearts and souls as much as our ears.

3. *Movement and Stillness*

> *Labyrinths are usually in the form of a circle with a*
> *meandering but purposeful path, from the edge to the*
> *center and back out again. Each one has only one path,*
> *and once we make the choice to enter it, the path*
> *becomes a metaphor for our journey through life.*
>
> —Lauren Artress, *Walking a Sacred Path*

> *I just put my feet in the air and move them around.*
>
> —Fred Astaire

Imagine you are the thirteenth-century Islamic mystic and poet Mevlana Jelaluddin Rumi walking through the dusty streets of a town in Turkey. Your beloved teacher Shams of Tabriz has disappeared and is possibly dead and your heart is heavy with grief. As you walk, however, the mundane sounds of the streets and the market place insinuate their way into your consciousness. The rhythmic harmony of the gold beaters hammering the sheets of gold, the marketplace laughter, the sound of rushing water, even the dogs barking—all resounding with the name *Allah*. With each step you take you repeat the name of Allah, Allah, Allah and the whole city seems to join your mantra.

A miracle happens. Instead of grief and worry, you are overcome with joy and lightness. You unfold your arms like a baby bird taking flight for the first time and you begin to whirl through the streets in ecstasy. People may stare and shake their heads, but you don't care. You have discovered the power of turning—the power of prayer inherent in your physical body that unites you with all creation, and thus with God.

As in all good legends, there is a tinge of incredibility to this one; the tale seems larger than life. Yet true or not, it has the kernel of a profound truth: through physical movement, humans can transcend the material world and take a step into the spiritual realm. Rumi had found another rhythmic key to ecstasy, a means of closing the gap separating us from God and easing the sense of loss and longing that plagues human kind. From this divinely inspired moment, Rumi began to incorporate turning and music into his already notable and mystic poetic rites. Thus some 700 years ago was born the Mevlevi Order of Dervishes, also known as the "whirling dervishes," quite possibly the most renowned and awe-inspiring religious dancers in the world.

Sadly, not all religions use movement to the same extent as the mystic order of whirling dervishes. Reverend Sharon Blackburn, senior minister of a Congregational church in Brooklyn, New York says some Christian churches are "stately, dignified—even stiff." She offers her own church as an example. "We don't have enough movement in our tradition. We stand up, sit down, kneel, in the average worship service," she says, and the choir and clergy perhaps take a few processional steps. "I wish we had more. At my installation here at Plymouth Church, I had someone do a modern dance," as part of the ceremony—a radical event that did not sit well with all members of the congregation.

On the other hand, the dervishes do not twirl completely alone on the cosmic dance floor. Many other traditions are moved by the spirit, as anyone knows firsthand if they've ever been to a gospel music service like those at Glide Memorial in San Francisco, where the rhythms are so powerfully moving—literally—that you cannot possibly contain yourself. Before you know it your hands will not stay demurely folded in your lap, the body simply will not stay glued to the pew because—YES!—the good Lord Himself has lifted you up and is making your hands fly together and apart, together and apart, and your hips—PRAISE JESUS!—are weaving a complex earthy pattern that is so basic to human needs and yearnings and joyfulness that it is simply the most recent step in a long trail of honoring God that leads all the way back to the Garden of Paradise—AMEN!

Clearly the body is a vessel for the soul, but it is also surely a vessel that was made for movement. The ultimate goal of movement in religious traditions is to bring us closer to God but—not so fast—there is a vast repertoire of interim steps along the way. Yes, we engage in physical movement when we spin ecstatically—and also when we kneel serenely in prayer, transport ourselves to our houses of worship, enact the rituals we cherish or undertake lengthy pilgrimages.

It is physical movement that enables us to labor the way God labored to create the world, and thereby savor the rewards and the sweet contrast of times of stillness, of rest. All of life is both dance and journey, with sacred pauses that may be as pregnant with meaning and purpose as are the movements. We are all pilgrims and dancers moving ever onward in a series of stops and starts, by turns graceful and awkward, slow and fast, seeking to move literally and figuratively closer to the One. Physical movement is both the vehicle and the symbol of that sublime inner movement. "We are all on a path," says Reverend Blackburn. And, in the overly sedentary world so many of us inhabit where it seems an effort just to get up to get the remote, physical movement is a way to get reacquainted with both our spiritual and earthly selves and find an inner place where they touch.

TRIP THE LIGHT FANTASTIC

In most traditions, sound birthed creation. But once created, does the universe passively listen to the sounds of the spheres? No! All of creation dances. Movement is everywhere, given shape, meaning and rhythm by rest: the blazing sun traversing the sky, the whistling wind in the trees, a bird in flight, a baby's curious reach, a loved one's tender caress, thoughts zipping through our heads, the rotation of the earth and the planets in their orbits and all celestial bodies on their paths to who knows where. Our bodies themselves, even when we sit or sleep, are cauldrons of activity—blood pumping, breath going in and going out, molecules flowing through the membranes of our cells. And in the invisible world of the subatomic level, matter is eternally engaged in a cosmic dance of life. Fritjof Capra writes that modern physics "has revealed that every subatomic particle not only performs an energy dance, but also *is* an energy dance—a pulsating process of creation and destruction." We are all dancers and we are the dance itself. We dance the dance of becoming, the story of our lives taking shape in grand and tiny steps, skips and twirls, twists and turns, in shimmies and shakes and great flying leaps, slow shuffles and languid shrugs.

Our gods and prophets were creatures of action; the original action heroes, they shaped the world with their hands, parted seas, led their people across vast wastelands and went on long pilgrimages themselves. Sometimes, they danced the world into existence. Shiva, the Hindu Lord of the Dance, created the world through dance, and also maintains it through dance. In an endless cycle of birth, death and rebirth that patterns the human cycle of reincarnation, Shiva will also dance the world to dissolution, only to dance it into existence again. In *Dance of Shiva*, A.K. Coomaraswamy describes Shiva's dance this way:

In the night of Brahman, nature is inert and cannot dance

until Shiva wills it. He rises from his rapture and, dancing, sends through inert matter pulsing waves of awakening sound, and LO! Matter also dances, appearing as a glory mound about him. Dancing, he sustains its manifold phenomena. In the fullness of time, still dancing, he destroys all forms and names by fire and gives new rest.

Just as the human voice was the first instrument of sound and music, the human body was the first medium of kinetic art. Watching our children, we watch early humans spontaneously dancing for joy, trembling with fear, shaking and stamping their feet in rage, imitating the sounds and movements around them, expressing what's inside as well as interpreting, deepening and integrating their experience of the world. In the poet Rumi's words, we celebrate and imitate and are one with "the waters which spring from their sources, the branches of trees which dance like penitents, the leaves which clap their hands like minstrels."

Psychologists and theologians theorize that dance evolved as a coping mechanism. They speculate that early humans knew movement was an effective safety valve to release the tension caused by the struggle for existence in a puzzling environment. (Much as we today release tension through dance, running and sports and express frustration, fear and anger through violence.) These spontaneous movements eventually became patterned and symbolic.

According to this theory, a people might, for example, do a dance requesting rain. If rain did fall soon after, then obviously the gods had been pleased by the particular movements performed. Voila: the Rain Dance. In the same way was born the Sun Dance, The Corn Dance and so on.

In *Dance as Religious Studies* Doug Adams writes that dance is a "natural expression of human beings from the earliest days through all civilizations, cultures and religions." Religious dances were a natural way for primitive peoples to express themselves and, according to Adams, "symbolic movement was probably the first of the arts since it required no material outside the human body."

The ancient Greeks believed that "dance was the art that most influenced the soul and provided the expressive way for that overflowing awareness for which there were no words." Plato wrote that all creatures express their emotions through movement (think of a happy tail-wagging puppy, or a contented cat rolling around on his back) and that we transform this instinct into dance thanks to the gods' gift of rhythm. Other Greeks believed dance was transmitted from the gods and therefore dancing was spiritual (an easier concept to grasp in those days when there were no boundaries between religious and worldly dance).

To this day, people dance to placate and entreat the gods. Often the object of desire is food or fertility or both. The Gogo of Tanzania perform an annual ritual for good rains and fertility. Parents of twins in Uganda are considered to be exceptionally fertile and dance in the gardens of their friends to transmit their fertility to their friends' garden crops. Men and women in Tanzania dance by moonlight in erotic rites wherein they embrace tightly and mimic sexual intercourse, an activity believed to promote fertility. Contrast this with the more contemporary and classic Western image of an unhappy, very pregnant woman lamenting, "I *should* have danced all night!" Dance as birth control? As we'll see, dance and movement are sometimes used as substitute for the horizontal mambo in certain traditions and circumstances. Dance, it seems, can either encourage or discourage fertility and hanky panky. Depending on your religion, it can be a gift from God or the work of the devil.

"TO REJOICE WITH THE WHOLE BEING"

As is the case with many faiths, young people complain that they find little relevance, little to attract them to worship services. Not true at B'nai Jeshurun, a synagogue on New York's Upper West Side, where every Friday night the beginning of the Sabbath is celebrated with song and dance. About midway through the service, all those who wish to dance rise and pour into the aisles, take hands, and form a smiling, laughing conga-like line. The dancers—of all ages, including young children on the shoulders of their elders—weave in and out, around and around, while the rest of the congregation sings and claps in a warm and joyous expression of Jewish soul. Although the hand clappers are participating in the service more than most people in most houses of worship, they are missing out on one of the dance's most comforting and enlivening aspects—touch. Clasping hands in a long line, you feel connected, plugged into the human energy running through the line like a current of electricity through a wire.

Marcelo Bronstein, one of the rabbis at "BJ's" as it is affectionately known, says, "We dance as part of our prayerful experience. The difference between BJ and other places is that we believe it is not enough to speak about the idea of God. Much of Judaism became too much of the head—an intellectual experience." This synagogue's service is about the experience of the divine. "You experience the divine," says Rabbi Bronstein, "when you choose not to be a spectator, and decide to participate and engage and take a risk." The dancing is a celebration, and it makes the service come alive more than any music and singing could do alone. It was not always thus; the lively dancing was sparked by a near tragedy. "Few people know that the dancing began spontaneously," explains Bronstein. The ceiling of the Moorish-style synagogue collapsed a few years ago, about one hour before the service was about to begin. Part of it landed on the pews and the pulpit, meaning one of the rabbis could have been killed or seriously injured, as well as some of the congregants. The whole congregation decided to move the service around the corner temporarily, to the school. "In the moment of an alleluia, out of joy and gratefulness that no one was hurt, people began to dance. And we haven't stopped dancing since."

Jewish faith has a long and rich history of dance as a way to praise God and express great joy for His blessings: "to rejoice with the whole being" according to Hebrew Scriptures. There are many references to dance in the Jewish Bible. For example, the book of Samuel describes the early prophets, who moved about in bands and whose prophecies required vigorous physical exercise. They played music and danced and whirled; their movements growing wilder and more abandoned until they were transported to a state of ecstasy. They embraced dance as a way to wonderfully concentrate the attentions more intensely and allow the dancer to return the body and the mind to God.

Dance embodies joy in religious and secular life alike in the Jewish tradition. In earlier times it was the custom to welcome the Sabbath on Friday before sunset with processions and dancing and the singing of Psalms. On Saturday worshipers danced a farewell to the parting Queen of Sabbath. There were also wooing dances and these were of course eventually followed by wedding dances in which rabbis and scholars danced to honor the bride. The Talmud commands dancing at weddings for both the bride and groom and their guests; in this setting dance symbolizes fruitful fulfillment of God's will to procreate, and is a mitzvah—a good deed performed for everyone—including yourself. The Israelites also held festive dances in celebration of the harvest and of holy days. Dance was communal and usually took the form of dancing in a circle and leaping, similar to the well-known folk dance called the *hora*.

Today, B'nai Jeshurun is the exception; most Jewish dancing is limited to holiday celebrations and in conjunction with rites of passage ceremonies such as weddings. "In most Jewish orders, movement is subtle," says Rabbi Leon Klenicki, director of interfaith affairs at the Anti-Defamation League in New York. He gives the example of men rocking rhythmically back and forth when they pray. Why do they do this? They are "playing with the words," he says, moving in time with them as they utter them silently, or softly, or loudly, so that "you feel that the prayer gets into your body."

Hasidic Jewish services are another exception; they emphasize individual expression of devotion. Dance is one vehicle for such personal expression, and they incorporate a form of ecstatic dance into their worship, with dance achieving mystic fervor particularly on Saturday nights. Improvised solo dances, arms raised and bodies assuming distinctive soulful postures and gestures connote intense, inspired communication with God. Hasidic dancing is often performed in a circle, which is symbolic of the Hasidic philosophy that everyone is equal and each is a link in the chain, the circle having no front and no back, no beginning and no end. It is the ultimate community dance, as most folk traditions know.

There are other less free-form approaches using dance as a creative way to teach and keep Jewish tradition alive. JoAnne Tucker is director of the Avodah Dance Ensemble, a professional New York-based modern dance company where repertory is inspired by Jewish ritual, liturgy and history. In 1990 she teamed up with Susan Freeman to write a book, *Torah in Motion*. The book contains dance improvisations or choreographed movements of over 100 specific passages of the Torah, called Dance Midrashim. The authors' goal is to help "dancers expand upon, explore, and, or bring the biblical verse into perspective." While the customary literary Midrash (in which the Torah is explained, interpreted, related to contemporary life and uses) helps bring the Bible to life, dance Midrash "enables us to interact closely with one another, thus heightening the social response and deepening the emotional experience. . . . Dance can be a significant and fostering retention of learning." In the foreword to the book, Rabbi Norman Cohen writes, "There's not a more dynamic art form by which to interpret the Bible than dance. The latent power of the narrative and often complex human interaction included in it can most vividly be captured by the movement and creative spontaneity of modern dance."

DANCING TOWARD ECSTASY

They are men and they are wearing skirts—big white skirts—that unfurl like the petals of a tulip as they whirl; slowly at first, then faster and faster for two, or three or more hours, a constant twirl up to God, to ecstasy. It may be hard to believe, but they are Muslims, albeit members of the unorthodox sect known as whirling dervishes. Although most of us can remember spinning in circles as kids, few if any of us claimed to see God in that thrillingly nauseating vertiginous vortex. Something must be happening when these Sufis dance that's more than meets the eye.

Perhaps the difference is discipline: the dervishes are finely honed products of dervish schools and years of mental, spiritual and physical training. "In a sense it is simply turning," explains Latif Bolat, Turkish-born musician and musical director of the Mevlevi Association of America. But it is challenging, too. "Just imagine turning nonstop for almost two hours. Without hard work, devotion and practice, it would be impossible for the dancers to turn for even two minutes." But once you get to a certain level of technical proficiency, "it is just ecstasy to turn," according to Bolat.

Another secret is that the dervishes close off their minds and open their hearts—a fundamental rule in whirling and Sufi mysticism in general. It is said that if you turn from your head, you will get dizzy. If you turn from your belly you will get sick. But if you turn from your heart, you will achieve ecstasy. It probably doesn't hurt that trance-like music accompanies the dance, and that the dervishes repeat a mantra as they twirl, a practice said to empty their hearts of all but the thought of Allah and enable them to "whirl in the ecstatic movement of His breath."

Dancing dervishes do not represent typical Muslim behavior.

"Islam did not have much to do with the expression of religious sentiments through artistic form other than geometrical designs and calligraphy," says Bolat; "singing, chanting, playing an instrument and dancing is not acceptable in Orthodox Islam." Alcohol and other consciousness altering drugs are also forbidden. That's why Sufism was born—a tradition that embraces Islam but that seeks a more direct and mystical knowledge of God.

"The whole idea of Sufism traditionally is to get into a trance. Depending on the sect, if getting into a trance required a drug such as hashish or wine, they did it," explains Bolat. The Mevlevi Sufi Sect, founded by Jelaluddin Rumi, prefers dance as a mind-altering medium—hence the name, whirling dervishes.

In its heyday, dervishes whirled barefoot in wooden *tekkes*, on floors worn mirror-smooth by their ceaseless footfalls. Every Thursday night the participants would meet for the sacred ceremony, called *sama*. The ceremony invokes intense love through prayer, poetry, music and turning, which is a metaphor for "turning to God." Rumi has described sama as

> the witnessing of the state of perceiving the mysteries of God through the heavens of divinity. Sama is to fight with one's self, to flutter, struggle desperately like a half-slaughtered bird, bloodstained and covered with dust and dirt . . . Sama is a secret . . . Sama is to attain that place where even an angel cannot go.

As they dance, the samazen turn from right to left, symbolic of turning to the heart. Their left foot is anchored to the ground, and their right foot propels them around and around. Their right hand extends upward to receive benevolent bounty and their left points to the earth. In this position, the dancer looks as though he is embracing an invisible Lover—which he is.

The sama consist of four *selams* or musical movements. They signify the acceptance of creation, the rapture of witnessing creation, the sacrifice of the mind to love and submission to God, which is accompanied by annihilation and transformation of the self. In the old days, the sheikh joined the dervishes in the fourth selam. He represented the sun, and the dervishes the planets turning around him, the solar system of *Mevlana*, the term of endearment for their founder Rumi.

The dervishes wear long black cloaks, which represent the tomb, and which they remove before twirling. Underneath they wear full white skirts, representing the spirit's shroud. On their heads are tall, honey-colored hats called *siklees*, which represent the spirit's tombstone. As they twirl, the skirts unfurl, a spectacular mesmerizing site. An observer has likened the effect to watching poetry, and the sight of men whirling can paradoxically make you feel very still.

What's it like to neutralize earth's glue and twirl oneself free from earthly bondage? Ira Friedlander gives us a glimpse when he quotes a twelve-year-old practitioner in his book, *Whirling Dervishes*: "Sometimes, during the sama, it feels as if Mevlana is holding my hand. I begin to smile inside, and my heart is warm, and later it is as if what my eyes see is different from before."

Today, the tekkes are gone, banished by Turkish Republic law 677 decreed in 1925, which also abolished the dervish orders. There are only private rites conducted by Lovers of Mevlana who have been trained in the old tradition. A government-sanctioned, tourist-pleasing form occurs Thursdays in Konya, in a large high school gymnasium. The samazen have tried to preserve the essence and tradition of the sama as much as possible. A large Turning Ceremony also occurs yearly in December and thousands of people attend to commemorate the death of Rumi.

Perhaps the whirling dervish performers will enjoy an increase in popularity at least in the West. Soon after Gerry Garcia died and the Grateful Dead stopped touring, Bolat

noticed new members in the audience during one of his concerts: Young people with dreadlocks. When he expressed his
curiosity to one of them, a young woman replied, "It's not so
weird . . . the best thing we used to do at the Dead concerts was
turning and whirling and getting high and this is the closest
music to that."

A DIFFERENT DRUMMER

The Shakers are a fascinating example of the ability of Christians
to absorb the paradox of the spirit-body separation that has shaped
Christian doctrine for centuries. Founded in 1747 and named after
their unique style of movement or dancing, Shakers otherwise held
the body at arm's length and were able to conceptually divorce the
spirit from the body. In fact, like the Hindu concept of using the
senses to transcend the senses, Shaker dance aims to transcend the
body by using the body in a set of specific dances. Shakers lived
celibate, austere, humble lives of hard physical work. However,
they indulged in ecstatic running, jumping, whirling and most of
all shaking—all designed to shake off the past sins, doubts and
faults, to mortify lust, and to stamp out evil. Thus free from such
encumbrances, they could turn over a new leaf. Some would point
out another benefit, common to sects where celibacy is exalted:
during a typical service, Shaker dances involved a buildup of energy that climaxed and then relaxed totally—a pattern of tension and
release not unlike that of sexual relations.

In an odd but wonderful little book called *A Shaker Service
Reconstructed*, J.G. Davies says that Shaker dancing caused "some
scandal" and that they spent a lot of energy defending this practice and explaining the reasons for it. Shakers said their form of
dancing is in accordance with Old Testament; it is a gift of God
and his gifts are to be used, not neglected. Worship should be
active and this means that the whole of one's body should be ded-

icated to the praise of God. Shaker dancing encourages unity and cooperation, recognizes and consecrates natural aptitudes and skills and affirms the equality of the sexes. Finally, since Christians are on a pilgrimage to the heavenly Jerusalem, they should be constantly on the march in the form of an ordered dance.

In the early days each Shaker moved spontaneously and with individual abandon. The movements were not choreographed. Eventually, however, the Shakers created elaborate patterns of movement. Feet became a percussion instrument (much like tap dancing is today, unbeknownst to most audiences). Shakers were encouraged to dance with "more forcible drumming of the feet," according to Davies, and "those who were limber jointed would bend their knees, till their fingers would almost or quite touch the floor." They rose on their toes and swung their arms horizontally from the elbows. Palms facing down they shook their arms. They held their hands in prayer position, they stretched their arms up and gazed heavenward, they mimed playing of the trumpet, harp, cymbals and plucked imaginary stringed instruments. As the older Shakers became less nimble dancers, the Sacred March was born, with "pacing with elastic steps, hands waving by the sides of the head and being clapped together." Although less physically rigorous, these were choreographically quite complex, and became known for their intricate floor patterns and contemporary accounts testify to the "skill in maneuvering" and "sense of tempo." Despite the orderly patterns of the feet and arms, spontaneity was preserved and even encouraged and Shakers were moved to shout "hosanna," "alleluia" and "more love!"

MIND OVER MATTER

Why should the Shakers prove to be so exceptional among Christiandom? Why isn't there more exuberant dance movement in our houses of worship? Blame it on sex. Movement involves the body: flesh, blood, bone, and often sweat, that indelicate indicator of body heat and passion. Not surprisingly, a religion's attitude toward the body in general colors the religion's attitude toward the body and its activities. Even though most religions encourage procreation, some get upset over the fact that this generally requires the act of sexual intercourse and bodily contact (although science is working to eliminate this step). The seemingly glorious ideal of creating more believers paradoxically clashes with a negative view of the means and material of achieving that holy goal.

Although we find mixed messages about the body and spirit in all three monotheistic religions, it is Christianity that has the most fascinatingly complex love-hate relationships with the flesh. On the one hand: flesh is great, the body is godly. Christ was the word (God) made flesh. The human body is a Temple for the Holy Spirit; the church is the Body of Christ. Christ said of the consecrated bread and wine, "Take, eat this is my body, this is my blood." In the Aramaic that Jesus spoke, "dance" and "rejoice" were the same word. Acts of John describe a "Hymn of Jesus" in which his disciples dance in a circle around Jesus. Early Christians took their cues from the Jews and felt that pious dancing revealed that a person physically felt the love of God. They regarded dance as a way for people to express their desire to get into heaven: Dancing on earth emulated the angels who were nonstop dancers, particularly on the heads of pins.

Through history, Christians have adored the inanimate physical manifestations of God and reveled in the caresses and kisses of ecstatic piety. Many of the medieval wooden sculptures of the Holy Family, particularly of Mary and Jesus, have been worn smooth, the details of their features and folds of their clothing rubbed into soft-edged ambiguity by hundreds of fervent fingertips and hot, passionate lips. This practice was encouraged by such writings as *Meditations on the Life of Christ*, which urged its readers to "Kiss the beautiful little feet of the infant Jesus who lies in the manger and beg his mother to offer to let you hold him awhile. Pick him up and hold him in your arms, gaze on his face with devotion and reverently kiss him and delight in him."

And yet, there is also running through Christianity a thread of dread of human flesh. They may call the body a Temple, but it too often is treated like an embarrassing, naughty, demanding child. What makes possible this repulsion is the notion of the separation of mind and body. The mind and the heart can remain pure, but flesh is the root of evil and thus a source of shame and humiliation. The world of the flesh must be transcended, its sins and temptations resisted, sometimes to the extremes of self-mortification by painful self-flagellation and the wearing of hair shirts. On the one hand Christianity espouses feverish caressing of Jesus statues and the effusive swaying jubilation of a Baptist gospel service (and how many Christians were swooning over the grinding pelvic passion of Elvis?); and on the other the ascetic celibacy of monks and the stiff-hipped purity of the Virgin Mary.

Amidst this theological tug of war for the hearts and bodies of Christians, religious dance struggled to survive. Through the early years of Christianity, sacred dance was regarded as a fusion of the spiritual with the physical. It was a natural way of expressing joy, a way to obtain holiness and salvation, a means of adoration. Many of the early Christians were converted pagans, and if there's one thing pagans love to do, it is dance. Unfortunately, many of these dances were ancient fertility dances, which were rather too unrestrained and sensual for the Church's taste. However, as Fred Astaire so exhuberantly belted out as he tapped, "Gotta Dance"— this is a sentiment that even applies to Catholic saints and priests. St. Teresa of Avila is said to have quite openly danced with holy joy. French priests danced the Pelota of Auxerre, a complex and rather bizarre dance form that combined the tossing of a ball with dancing around a labyrinth. Christians danced to Christmas carols, and mothers danced around the altar with babies in their arms.

Christian liturgy and Bible stories apparently were just too innately theatrical and theater and dance were a potent communications combination, especially for the masses, who could neither read nor afford books. Church as entertainment and education reached rather elaborate heights: dramatic performances involving both dancing and processionals were staged at Christmas and Easter, and also saints' days and festivals. Mumming at Christmas became popular (and still is in parts of the United Kingdom and North and South America). Mystery, miracle and morality and Passion plays took place in churchyards, and it was common for people to dance at funerals and at the graves of family, friends and martyrs as a way to deny death as well as comfort the dead and facilitate resurrection. Pageants with *tableaux vivants* of Bible scenes were popular, communicating wordlessly through gesture and pose.

With the rediscovery of classical antiquity of the Renaissance came a new kind of dance based on ancient Greek traditions and philosophy. Dances consisted of simple steps and elaborate spatial patterns that have been likened to those of a marching band at today's football games. It seems Busby Berkeley would have been proud, as dancers formed geometrical floor patterns that seamlessly morphed one into the next. But instead of spectacle for spectacle's sake, these formations were highly symbolic—the changeability of the patterns represented the inconstancy of nature along with the grand unifying order of God. The patterns themselves symbolized the harmony and cycles of nature, as well as order and virtue. Orderly dancing was said to cultivate order within the souls of the dancers and observer alike. The Jesuits were a somewhat surprising advocate of dance and movement. Always the educators, this order of the Christian Church took advantage of the stage and used visual spectacle including "biblical ballets" to indoctrinate the masses in Europe and the New World.

After the Renaissance, dance as a form of religious expression faded. For one thing, the mind ascended in importance as the emphasis shifted to the intellect. The Protestant Reformation, with its starched, white-collar, stiff-upper-lip Calvinism and Puritanism, banned dances and processions except for funeral processions. The Christian Church's dancing days were over, as both Roman Catholic and Protestant churches limited physical expression to the movements of the mass itself. Christians were busted, grounded, like naughty teenagers who were having too much fun for their own good. This prevailing negative view of dance persisted strongly and tested the boundaries between church and state when the US was moved to enact "blue laws" that prohibited dancing of any kind on Sundays.

MOVING PRAYER AND MEDITATION

Orthodox Muslims may not dance either, but their entire lives are shaped by the five-times-a-day prayer called *salat*. Salat does not involve just words—it is "a devotional heart-surrender with physical motion," according to Coleman Barks in *The Illuminated Prayer*. The prayer action is preceded by The Ablutions: washing of the hands, mouth, nose, face, eyes, feet. This washing "gives you time, bit by bit, part by part, to move your awareness away from the world and toward God," writes Barks. Even before beginning the actual salat, the worshiper is using movement to enter a sacred space and time.

Typically, the Muslim hears the mellifluous Arabic call of the *mezzuen* (once called by a live person, but now most often by a recording). He turns toward the direction of Mecca, and steps onto the prayer mat, his refuge where the demands and cares of life lose their grip. The graceful rhythmic movements that follow are "an accompaniment to the prayer, they are the prayer itself, a mysterious flow of form through which God praises God."

Each time of day has its own number of prayer cycles or

rakkats, said aloud, in silence or a combination of the two. Each cycle consists of the verbal prayer said with the body in a certain position, and each position has its own meaning and purpose. When you stand with hands raised, the palms open and facing forward, you express receptivity to the Divine presence. When you clasp the hands over your abdomen, you acknowledge a powerful energy center. Bowing at the waist, hands resting on the knees, your body enjoys its "first taste of submission." Dropping to the knees and placing the forehead and hands on the floor is "the moment of surrender." Kneeling, palms on thighs, encourages you to probe your inner psyche and ask for forgiveness. The final posture is the heart embrace—the gentle embracing of fellow worshipers, seeing and feeling "the radiance of God within another."

Why pray five times a day? Muslims believe that there are five elemental forces, or primordial elements: earth, fire, water, air and ether. Each element rules certain mental and emotional energies and exerts its strongest influence at a certain time of day, a belief shared with Hindus. Therefore, the prayers are done at these times because that is when it is "most effective in transforming these elemental forces."

In addition, the daily sun cycle is seen as a mirror of the human life span, which consists of five stages during which "the soul makes its journey around another sun that never rises or sets." "Aligning devotional work with these natural times of power, we start to move with the rhythms of God's creation in a new way, attuned to the mystical correspondences between outer and inner and to the seasons of life," according to Barks.

The salat may be the most specifically choreographed prayer in the world, but the gestures that comprise it—bowing, bending, kneeling, prostration—are "archetypal motions and gestures that appear in endless variation throughout all the devotional practices of the human family," says Barks. How true. Gestures in worship services all over the world are often simple and often involve the hands, the most versatile and expressive part of the body for the job. When you look up at the ceiling of the Sistine Chapel, you see the finger of God giving the spark of life to the eloquently extended hand of Adam. When you go to a Christian service, the priest, with his hand, makes the sign of the cross to bless you, sprinkles holy water and anoints with precious oil or other liquids. Every tradition ministers to the sick by the laying on of hands, a very comforting and healing sensation known as Therapeutic Touch when it is taught formally to nurses in hospitals. We wash our hands to purify us of sin and worldliness, we wash our feet and those of others. These we do out of respect, reverence, and humility, and in their simplicity they can speak more than words could ever convey.

Gestures are so powerful that Hinduism and Buddhism have a complex vocabulary of sacred hand gestures called *mudras*. Often used to "seal" the efficacy of a mantra, prayer or other religious act, they are the wordless equivalent to Captain Picard's "make it so." Another type of mudra serves as markers of identity in statuary and paintings. The most familiar one is the gesture that means "do not fear": the right hand is held up, palm facing outward. Christ also made this gesture, as a sign of benediction and peace. We all know at least one mudra: hands in prayer position. Try it now—place your palms together, center them over your chest, fingers pointing upward, and hold it for a few breaths. Do you feel more centered, more balanced, calmer and more at peace?

This simple gesture is referred to as "namaste" in the discipline of yoga. "The idea of yoga is to still the body and still the mind," says Rachel McDermott, assistant professor of Asian and Middle Eastern cultures at Barnard College. Hatha yoga, a profound and accessible form of physical movement is a series of challenging movements or positions of the physical body that are used to prepare the mind and body for long periods of meditation and to support a spiritual life, says McDermott. Many people who study this physical form of yoga are initially interested because it is extremely relaxing and keeps you fit and limber. But as they go deeper into the practice, if they have a good teacher, they find yoga is much, much more. Yoga can itself become a "moving meditation." It is a great teacher of patience, tolerance, discipline, honesty and self-knowledge. Cumulatively the poses and the breathing are said to affect the "subtle body"—the energy pathways and pools through which circulate the life force.

THE LONG AND WINDING ROAD

Oddly enough, in many traditions, movement on a grand scale is more common than modest movement in a house of worship. The grand pilgrimage is an ancient custom in all of the major world religions, and people have long felt the need to journey at least once in their lifetimes to a holy place. Christians go to Rome, Jerusalem, Lourdes, Turin, Fatima or any of a zillion lesser saintly shrines. Luxurious buses leave every Lenten season from Queens and Manhattan for the Shrine of the Divine Mercy in Stockbridge, Massachusetts (Round-trip fare: $30. Cash only. No refunds. Bring your own lunch.)

The Crusades also were a kind of pilgrimage, but the less said about them the better. Judaism has three annual festivals connected with pilgrimages to Jerusalem: Passover, Shavuot and Sukkot. These mark a stage in the agricultural year but each is also a progressive step toward true freedom and spiritual maturity.

"The idea behind a pilgrimage is that you spend time, money and energy," says Father Cormier, associate pastor of St. Rose of Lima Parish in New Jersey. In many places, such as Germany, France, Spain and Portugal, pilgrimages involve a lot of walking. "People want to be tired because it indicates that you are making an effort, that you are giving something significant to God." Cormier reminds us that simple steady walking is a tremendously universal spiritual tradition. The rhythm of the repetitive motion of putting one foot in front of the other helps us "get in the groove" and closer to God.

Processions, which resemble mini-pilgrimages, are part of many festivals and worship services. For example, Pastor Cormier's parish is comprised of a largely Latin population and in Latin countries and cultures the Good Friday procession is a major event. His parish stages the procession come hell or high water; in fact being uncomfortably drenched by rain "is a plus." Some dress as bad guys, some as Roman soldiers and someone takes on the role of Jesus and carries a huge cross through the streets of Newark. "I did it myself once," Pastor Cormier says, and "its heavy, it hurts," as it must have hurt Jesus. Thousands participate in the procession, which takes a couple of hours. "We march and stop, march and stop, pausing at the fourteen stations of the cross—neighbors' homes representing the fourteen things that happened to Jesus on the last day of his life—and read fourteen messages in three languages. In this way, people get to experience the passion of Christ."

All able-bodied Muslims are obligated to make the pilgrimage or *hajj* to Mecca at least once in their lives. The hajj is one of the Five Pillars of Islam and, in the past this grand gesture was an arduous journey for all Muslims. One struggled, traveling for years by caravan through the Sahara Desert, to reach the sacred city. Today, jets and government cooperation have made the journey easier, and airports in the Middle East, North Africa and Southeast Asia are crowded with passengers to Saudi Arabia.

The pilgrimage is a mass commemoration of the story of Abraham and the lessons it teaches. The pilgrim prepares beforehand by cleansing the soul by abstaining from hunting, sexual intercourse, angry words or obscenities. Once there, he dresses all in white. He follows a series of rites and treks to holy places. Pilgrims migrate to the plain of Arafat, thirteen miles southeast of Mecca, where there are prayers and a sermon in the often-broiling midday sun, as sins are washed away in a wave of mercy for those who are truly repentant. Prayer continues until sunset. Then the entire throng, which is nearly equal in number to the population of Houston, Texas, goes on the move again. They spend the night camping on an open plain, praying and resting, and perhaps gathering pebbles which they will cast the next day at one of three stone pillars.

The main activity is to walk seven times around the Kaaba, the shrine located at the center of the Great Mosque. This shrine is said to have been built by Abraham, and is revered as the holiest place on earth. While walking around the Kaaba, the pilgrim stops to kiss the black stone embedded in one corner, a stone believed to have been given to Adam when he was expelled from the Garden of Eden.

Hindus, with their multiple deities, naturally have many temples and other sacred sites to visit. The four corners of India—Badrinatha, Dwarka, Rameswaram and Puri—are said to be where the Hindu gods dwell and thousands visit them each year. The country's seven rivers are also sacred sites, with the Ganges being the all time favorite place to bathe and wash away spiritual impurities which, Westerners might call sins. The sacred body of water begins from the foot of the god Vishnu, flows across the sky as the Milky Way and comes down to earth through the hair of the god Shiva. The place it comes to earth is in the highest mountains on earth, the Himalayas; from here it flows down to India. Every twelve years people flock to Allahabad, on the Ganges, where they engage in a great ritual bathing fair.

AND ON THE SEVENTH DAY . . .

It may seem odd to advocate inactivity at a time when only twenty-five percent of us get enough exercise to be healthy, when thirty percent of us are on a weight-loss diet at any given moment, and when even our children are getting fatter and are reluctant to walk just a few blocks. And yet, amidst this sedentary existence, almost everyone suffers from too much activity—a busyness that is mostly of the mind. Although some of us may rush around, darting from one place and thing to another, it is not the physical effort that is causing the burn out and stress from which so many of us suffer.

"Many people are rushed, nobody has enough time for anything," observes Rabbi Irvin Ungar. Indeed, University of Maryland sociologist John Robertson has found a progressive increase in how hurried people feel: in 1965, twenty-five percent of those surveyed said their lives were rushed all the time; in 1992, researchers put the figure at thirty-eight percent, almost a fifty percent increase from 1965. Surprisingly, those who lived in small towns felt as rushed as those who lived in big cities. And both town and city dwellers felt their lives were hurried at both work and play. You don't need a special degree to see that something is terribly wrong here. Can an idea as old as the Sabbath, the biblical day of rest, help us get off the treadmill?

Pastor Cormier has given the problem a lot of thought. He believes mental fatigue is the root cause of much of the epidemic of depression in the modern world. "Life, especially in our complex modern society, takes a lot of mental energy. We are mentally tired, and [when this happens] almost everything provokes confusion, fear or sadness." This causes panic and panic uses up even more energy, causing a vicious cycle and driving us into a "deep dank hole where we suffer very much for nothing." To avoid the cycle, we need to allow ourselves to rest. We need to stop the imbalanced rhythm of a life in which we "go to work, work, get home from work, become busy with many things, go to bed, fall asleep, get up, go to work" and so on. Pastor Cormier sums it up this way:

One day connects with the next. We burnout, our faith becomes confused, and life becomes joyless and burdensome. When we are relentlessly busy on Saturday and Sunday, we have let our weeks connect. If we do not observe holidays and holy days, we have let our months connect too. If we do nothing special in the summer, we have let our years connect. None of this is a good idea.

Rabbi Irvin believes that "today more than ever" we need the Sabbath. This includes our clergy—one of the clergy interviewed for this book was ordered by her physician to slow down because her blood pressure had climbed dangerously high. Stephan Bertman of the University of Windsor in Canada has written a book called *Hyperculture: The Cost of Human Speed.* In it, he characterizes us as living in a society spinning wildly out of control and rushing perilously away from the values, rituals, sacredness and simple joys essential to health and healing. "This speed has become the yardstick by which we assign value, undermining the value of experiences and activities that require slowness to develop: psychological maturation, the building of meaningful and lasting human relationships to doing careful and responsible work, the creation and appreciation of the arts, and the research for life's greatest problems and mysteries." Bertman believes that our hyperculture "obscures the need to cultivate those skills and virtues—patience, commitment, self-denial and even self-sacrifice—without which no civilization can long endure."

We all need time out. Taking a real lunch hour, making time for ourselves in the evening after work, taking a well-deserved vacation—all can help. But to restore the things Bertman is talking about, we need more than just Time Out. We need quality time to reflect, to renew our perspective, to preserve history and family memories, to join with loved ones in shared traditions and rituals, to capture a sense of what is natural, enduring and true, to feel the presence of God. Although we need time away from work and mundane responsibilities, Bertman is talking about something more. Something that only the Sabbath, or something like the Sabbath, can provide.

But what is the Sabbath, exactly? "And He rested on the seventh day." This simple biblical passage seems straightforward enough. The Sabbath is a rest day. But the Sabbath is more than a cessation of labor. "Each week we stop time in order to recover time," says Rabbi Klenicki. "And also we celebrate creation, and family life." Stop time? Recover time? Control time when it seems to be controlling us? Is this possible?

In his elegant meditation, *The Sabbath: Its Meaning for Modern Man*, Abraham Joshua Heschel offers his deeply considered and poetic observations on this sacred day of rest. The Sabbath is "spirit in the form of time" and an opportunity to "stand still and embrace the presence of an eternal moment." It is an ancient idea that the Sabbath and eternity are one; that this Day of Days is an example of the world to come. If antiquity and Heschel are right, one-seventh of our lives can be spent in Paradise.

How can we create paradise on earth? By sanctifying time. Six days a week time and work rule our lives. We "wrestle with the world, wringing profit from the earth," Heschel says. In spite of timesaving devices, we frantically try to catch up; we are slaves to time just as Jews were slaves to the Egyptians thousands of years ago. He urges us to "lay down the profanity of clattering commerce . . . say farewell to manual work and learn to understand the world has already been created and will survive without the help of man." By taking time out we finally gain control over time. We create our own "architecture of time," a "cathedral of eternity" and experience a spiritual presence, which is the heart of the Sabbath. As we shift our attention from material things and the rushed feeling of the workaday world to the immateriality of time, the character of time changes palpably. It becomes holy.

Sabbath is not an interlude; it's a culmination, just as it was for God. We don't take this day of rest for the sake of increasing productivity during the other six days, although this may of course be a welcome little by-product. We take it for the sake of rest itself. We work so we can rest and enjoy the beauty of the oasis in time that the Sabbath provides. God decreed that labor is divine and it is also our destiny. God worked—he created the universe, but on the seventh day he rested. Adam had a job; he was the first gardener: "And the Lord God took the man, and put him into the Garden of Eden to dress it and keep it." (Genesis 2:15) So although part of the covenant with God is to work—and to love work—another part of the covenant is to abstain from work on the seventh day. That day belongs to God, not to work; he made it holy, and so should we—in fact he commands us to. In so doing, we create a bond of commonality with God. We celebrate our own work by stopping it as we celebrate God's.

What is work? What is rest? For the most traditional in the Jewish community, Sabbath, or Shabbat, means the complete cessation of all ordinary work-related activities including driving, cooking, building, buying, selling and writing. More liberal interpretations allow social and recreational activities. Heschel tells us that "labor is a craft, but perfect rest is an art." The Sabbath is not just a day of prohibition or austerity—thou shalt not do this or that—but a day of delight in the pleasures of the soul and body. Deuteronomy 3:1 tells us our pleasure will be rewarded:

> Sanctify the Sabbath by choice meals, by beautiful garments; delight your soul with pleasure and I will reward you for this very pleasure.

We not only abstain from physically engaging in work, but we don't even think or talk about it. We eschew unpleasant emotions too—no fire may be kindled, not even fiery anger. We abstain from noisy acts so we can hear the still and silent song that is the Sabbath. We must give it all our attention, so that we are worthy of it, the most precious gift among the many that God has bestowed upon us.

The ideal Shabbat begins on Friday at sundown and ends Saturday at sundown. Traditionally, you go to synagogue for services before dinner. But before services, observance begins at home with a symbolic welcoming of Shabbat: reciting blessings over candles, which the woman of the household, dressed in her finest, usually kindles. After the service, back at home the Kiddush (meaning "sanctification") is recited, with the blessing over the wine and the Sabbath itself observed. You also bless a special braided bread called *challah* and which represents the *manna*, which miraculously appeared to the Jewish people while they were wandering through the desert. Then you eat a special festive meal at a table set with a fine tablecloth, good dishes (specially for Shabbat) and silverware, perhaps fresh flowers. After dinner, it's time to sit back, enjoy conversation, sing a few Shabbat songs and give thanks.

Saturday morning you may attend another synagogue service and enjoy another "no work" leisurely but festive meal with blessings. The afternoon might be spent socializing with friends, perhaps taking a nap, or simply in quiet contemplation. At sundown, you perform the *Havdala* at home or at the synagogue. This ceremonial farewell to the day involves wine, sweet-smelling spices, a braided candle and a short service. As the fragrance of the spices linger, you are reminded of the peace of Shabbat and hope that this peace will spread to the world.

Like any religious holiday, observing the Sabbath regularly helps parents share time and values with their children. But like most worthwhile endeavors, it is not necessarily easy. Both Rabbi Klenicki and Rabbi Ungar recall what a struggle it was even for them to convince their children to keep the Sabbath. Ungar says,

Sabbath helps you teach kids what's important. Many of them would rather be out playing video games. But there isn't a Friday night that goes by that we don't light the candles, say the blessing over the wine, have a meal together. We have couples over to our home, and they say, "We wish our kids were with us." Of course, there were battles. Of course sometimes we yield. But the Sabbath sets up a structure—without that, who knows when we would be having a meal together?

"When one is young," says Rabbi Klenicki, "one wants to go the movies on Friday night, or play football, or go to a Friday night dance." His daughter used to complain that their Jewish neighbors let their daughter go to the dance, so why couldn't she? "I said it was because our neighbors wanted their children to be good Americans, which meant going to the Friday dance. But we are committed as Jews." Rabbi Klenicki's daughter is now raising her own family. Her father says, "She said to me recently that she is very grateful we were so strict with her. She says she's learned a good lesson, she has realized that the Sabbath is a very important time in your inner life and she is struggling now to pass on the tradition." And what if dance was introduced into the celebrations, as it was in ancient times and as it is at B'nai Jeshurun today? Perhaps there wouldn't be such "battles" with young people looking for relevance and meaning.

Not all traditions have a Sabbath, or anything like it. And many Jews ignore it, or have come to observe it haphazardly. What kind of world would it be if Sabbath were as commonplace as the forced merriment of the alcohol-sodden "Happy Hour?" Klenicki admits, "Shabbat is a challenge throughout your whole life—many people prefer the rushed rhythm of the work week. For many people it is difficult to be alone and quiet with yourself. It's very sad."

Saturdays and Sundays have become a time of shopping, of waiting for the next big sale, rather than contemplating God.

Ironically, the Sabbath helps us free ourselves of the shackles of want and coveting material things and replaces them with a longing for the bodily pleasures and soul-ennobling spirituality of the Sabbath day. Every day of our lives can be a pilgrimage to the seventh day, each day can be spiritually consistent with the Sabbath, and full of desire for that point in time that is the Sabbath. The Sabbath reminds us that material things seem permanent but in actuality are temporary and perishable. Time, which seems evanescent and always marching on, is in actuality infinite and everlasting. The Sabbath isn't quite time travel, but time suspension. It is the dimension in which we meet God and can sense the unity of all things.

Heschel asks, "Is there any institution that holds greater hope for man's progress than the Sabbath?" It sounds so simple. To set aside one day a week in which we can be free and be with ourselves, our family, our Creator. To unplug our phones and cease our worship of technological innovation and instruments which have become weapons of destruction. To stop spending (or making) money and to remove ourselves from our economic struggle with other people and our struggle to control nature. Simple? Yes. Easy? No.

A MOVING EXPERIENCE

It's 700 years since the dervishes began to whirl, 200 years since the Shakers began to shake, thousands of years since the first yogis sat in lotus position, thousands of years since the Torah urged us to change gears. Science now tells us that a balance of physical activity and rest is good for mental, social, and physical health. Exercise reduces the risk of overweight, fatigue and many serious conditions including heart disease, certain types of cancer, diabetes and osteoporosis. It sharpens the mind. Yoga improves balance and flexibility, reducing the risk of falls and

injuries. Adequate rest and vacations have been shown to be necessary for optimum health and productivity. The endorphins
released during vigorous movement such as dancing act as the
body's natural morphine, improving mood and lifting depression. You may or may not agree with Karl Marx when he said
religion is the opiate of the masses; but few would disagree that
dancing is the opiate of religion.

Dancers say that when they dance, they learn—about their
bodies, themselves and their place in the universe. As you dance,
everything comes together, including the bits and pieces of yourself that you have been ignoring or thought were lost. With an
open mind, any kind of dance can be a religious experience—any
kind of movement, if done deliberately and thoughtfully can be a
prayer. Fitness as a religion has become a joke, but some people do
get these moments of transcendence and wholeness in an aerobics
class. The music, the beat, the people breathing and sweating and
moving in sync create a powerfully meaningful experience where
you can go to a deep place of connection and joy.

That a balance of movement and stillness should be good for
our physical health in addition to our spiritual well-being is the
icing on the cake.

Or it may be another instance of God Himself moving in
mysterious and wonderful ways.

4. *Light and Darkness*

God answers all our prayers. Sometimes the answer
is yes. Sometimes the answer is no. Sometimes
the answer is you've got to be kidding!
—Jimmy Carter, 1997 Larry King interview

In a dark time, the eye begins to see.
—Theodore Roethke

As the world came horrifyingly close to annihilation by weapons of mass destruction, as we were living one heartbeat from blinding fireballs capable of triggering a long, dark, dreary, suicidal nuclear winter, many were at work behind the scenes. Some would say, the Light of the World prevailed. And who knows? Perhaps the prayer candles lit all over the world had their intended effect. You would not have a hard time convincing those who attend a small but delicately beautiful church near Taos, New Mexico. There, we find a candle, its steady flame a magnet for the eye amidst the cacophony of colorful idolatry in the softly lit apse. The candle itself is quite ordinary—plain white, housed in a glass cylinder. Its flame is, however, anything but ordinary: this little spark has circled the globe. It is called the Flame of Peace and it is suffused with hope and life.

The Santuario de Chimayo is the flame's permanent home but not the place of its birth. It originally blazed on the torch that was carried around the world in the First Earth Run in 1986, the United Nation's International Year of Peace. Every year since then, this modest beacon of humankind has been used in the Prayer Pilgrimage for Peace, carried by runners who also bear a packet of the sacred soil from the Santuario. At the birth-place of nuclear weapons—Los Alamos, New Mexico—both flame and soil are used in a Native American blessing conduct-ed in the spirit of healing, reconciliation and peace. A nearby sign tells us that the flame represents the "good" fire of God's love, which the people of God are called to share with one another and with all creatures on Planet Earth.

World Peace? God's Love? A heavy burden for such a plain-Jane candle to bear, but a potent reminder that 'tis better to light one candle than to curse darkness. And a powerful symbol, as well, particularly when paired with the dark soil. Think about it: Which do you prefer? A room streaming with sunlight or a dark, dank cave? At lunch, do most workers jockey for position in the shade or the sunny side of the park, faces uplifted to soak up its glorious radiance? Do blossoms open at sunset, or unfurl at dawn's golden rosy light? Mostly, we are drawn to the dancing lick of fire and light like a moth to a flame.

Light, as Martha Stewart would say, is a good thing. We have come to equate it with day, spirit, heaven, goodness, joy, life, knowledge and the Divine. In our religious lives, we use light in temples, churches, altars, near holy images and in processions. We light candles and fires on special occasions, layer our icons with gossamer leaves of gold, embed glowing stained glass win-dows in our houses of worship, endow our gods and saints with halos. Darkness on the other hand, is not so good. It symbolizes night, matter, earth, evil, despair, death, ignorance and the demonic. If we are lucky and diligent, we may become "enlightened." If, like most people, we are not, we stay "in the dark."

But wait. If we think further, we also realize that it is possible to have "too much of a good thing." Light can give us vision but it also can blind us. In the form of heat, it can warm us or burn us. Humans have harnessed fire and light, but we don't always use it wisely: consider the bright flash and deadly mushroom cloud that Los Alamos represents. And is darkness really so evil and undesirable? The dark, the night, may be frightening but, it is half of the rhythm of life. It offers soothing respite from the intense flame of the sun. So it is fitting that the New Mexico peace ceremony uses both flame and earth—the light and the dark. Both are aspects of the universal reality and of human nature.

With this mixed message in tow, moving from darkness to light is at the heart of many spiritual practices. From the brilliance of the salvation-flavored paschal candle emerging in a devilishly-darkened church at Easter to the exquisitely balanced and neutral-flavored black and white swirl of the traditional symbol for yin-yang, religion has sought to make sense of the paradoxes of the contrasting concepts of light and dark. The question remains: Can we make peace in life and in worship with both poles of existence—or must they wage war against each other until one wins out?

LIGHT IS LIFE

What is light, anyway? What is darkness? Much thought has been given to the first question, and the second is usually answered simply: "The absence of light." Regardless of the source, the miracle of light is a form of subtle energy fluctuations—vibrations in the electromagnetic field. Like sound, light is a primal energy from which all life on earth emerged, and upon which all life still depends. Science tells us that the universe began as a brilliant fireball, and that before the Big Bang all the light of the universe was compressed to a point tinier than the tip of a needle. Up to 700,000 years after that momentous event, matter did not exist; all was radiant energy, ten million times denser than matter.

In the Bible, light was the first thing that God created, and it was created out of darkness. In his book *Living Judaism*, Rabbi Wayne Dosick relates a marvelous old Jewish legend. Before creation, God's light filled the whole universe. When he decided to create the world, he had to make space for things—land, ocean, trees, birds, fish and so on. So he breathed in some of the divine light, and transferred it into some jars. Creation proceeded apace, all was well and God was pleased. The problem was (and there's always a problem—otherwise, there's no story) the jars could no longer contain all the energy of God's divine radiance. God's light burst out of the jars, shattering them into millions of little shards, and the light that had been in them broke into millions of little sparks. The shards fell to earth and became the ills and evils of the world. And each spark of God's light became a human soul. Both light and soul are pieces of God, and it is our job on earth to collect the shards of evil, to make them whole again and repair the hurts of the universe.

Similarly, many scientists believe that once the earth was formed, sunlight was the spark of life, the trigger for the primal chemical reactions that were the first baby steps toward life on this planet. Almost every living earthly thing still depends directly or indirectly on light, partly because of its crucial role in photosynthesis (*photo* means "light"), the process used by plants to produce food energy.

Look around. See that exquisitely formed rose? Can you smell its heady perfume? Without light there would be no soft petals, no perfume. See that sexy red sports car with the automatic sunroof? It's powered by fuel created millions of years ago by sunlight. What about that wooden crucifix? Made from a tree that needed sunlight to survive. Look in the mirror. That's right: you not only need sunlight to avoid bumping into rosebushes and roadsters, you need the plants that grow under its energetic glow to clean your air and fill your bowl.

The energy of light, directly and indirectly, feeds us. It also allows us to see, making it easier to find, cook and eat food, and do most of the other things we do in life. Sight gives us a form of information that our other senses don't. We don't really "see" an object; rather, the light bouncing off its surface enters our eyes, sending a signal to the brain for interpretation. There is no "red" or "blue" or "green" or "purple" in the material world— only a particular vibration energy our brain learns to interpret and give a name.

But the light of nature is not just sunsets and rainbows, moonbeams and falling stars, the glint of gold and diamonds, a bowl of granola, a bit of the grape. At the deepest level, the wisdom of both the ages and quantum physics suggests that we don't merely *need* light energy to survive. Rather, we *are* energy beings, made up of the vibrations and oscillations of light and sound. Scientists tell us that the universe is mostly light—for every single atom of matter, there are one billion particles of light, making matter "just a minor pollutant in a universe made of light," according to one physicist. In fact, your body stores enough light energy to illuminate a baseball field for three hours with one million watts of floodlights.

This notion is very similar to ancient Chinese philosophy and to Ayurveda, the Hindu health system based on 6,000-year-old sacred texts. Nutrition, in a sense, is everything we absorb into our body-mind-spirit: You are what you eat. Light, therefore, is itself a nutrient for health and rejuvenation; your body, mind and spirit need those photons or light particle waves, as much as a good meal or breath of air.

SACRED FIRE AND FLAME EVERLASTING

Light and its shadowy partner, darkness, have come to play vast and various roles in all the religious traditions, myths and cultures. Both have positive and negative functions and are inherently paradoxical. Sometimes religious doctrine makes a distinction between the invisible fire or light, or radiance—the vital force, the spark of life—and the material sources of light—sun, fire, moon, stars, soft white light bulbs. And sometimes it does not. Sometimes it recognizes the contradictory qualities in light and darkness and sometimes it does not. But it almost always prefers the former to the latter.

As Father Cormier, associate pastor of the St. Rose of Lima Parish in Newark, New Jersey points out, "Light is considered to be a virtue—in the light of faith you can see things better, with more truth, clarity and love. Dark is also a virtue, for example, during meditation, to take away distractions. But in the dark, you also can't see well, you stumble."

Throughout prehistory, history and even into the present, first the sun and then fire have functioned as our primary source of light and energy. So it's no stretch really to understand how light became associated with good and its absence with good's opposite. Sun and flame are givers of vision and life, capable of miraculously transforming substances. When darkness falls, poof! Life becomes unpredictable. We are naturally, primordially, appallingly and predictably fearful of the dark, wary of "things that go bump in the night." Life may have been precarious during the day in ancient times, but at least you could see the danger and have a fighting chance. At night, who knew what was out there, lurking, waiting to pounce on you and your innocent children clinging to you, wide-eyed with fear? Seasonal changes also wreaked havoc on our safety and satiety, as the diminishing sun brought the cold and with it the scarcity of food.

How little times have changed. Although few people in the industrial world suffer greatly from seasonal changes, the dark is still a universal creepy zone (except for musicians and other night crawlers). Instead of fires and torches we have streetlights, flood-lights, flashlights and night-lights to keep the demons at bay.

So, sun and fire (which the ancients saw as a piece of the sun) became sacred and magical. Sun and fire were worshipped with the awe and wonder and fear they deserved. Many turned them into gods, or their gods took on the attributes of sun and fire: light and heat. How life must have changed when humans learned to manipulate and then create fire! Life and fire became so intimately intertwined—every tribe and household had its own fire, its own hearth—that when someone died, the house-hold fire was also extinguished. Making and tending the fire was the female domain, as was cooking and making the home warm and light. As time went by, women—especially virgins—became keepers of the sacred flame as well.

All fires were not created equal. In many religious traditions, there is the "perpetual fire," which is purer, and the "new fire," kin-dled conscientiously and with awe. The candle at the Santuario de Chimayo is an example of perpetual fire, as is the eternal flame burning at Jewish and Christian altars, the Tomb of the Unknown Soldier in Paris and the flame lit for the Olympic Games—a flame that since 1936 has been kindled from a fire in Olympia.

India likely wins the prize for the most complex set of beliefs and rituals relating to fire. According to the Hindu worldview, fire is one of the five elements that constitute all things in existence. Hindus early understood the fascinating set of contradictory prop-erties of fire—its capacity to bring pleasure or pain; to give life or consume it. It symbolizes intelligence and the glow of health and the energy of passion, anger and lust. Fire also is the medium of purification. In Hindu ritual, there are three types of fire—heavenly fire, or the sun, which resides with the gods; atmospheric fire, or the moon, which resides with the ancestors and earthly fire or the domestic flame that resides with people. Fire has a starring role in Indian rituals, from everyday domestic and temple worship to marriage and funeral rites. Hindus believe the fire of cremation destroys, purifies and reconstitutes the old self to produce the new self. The banned practice of *sati*, in which the wife joined her husband on the funeral pyre, is said to symbolize the passage of the complete "sacrificial unit" of husband and wife into the next world; however, according to Dr. Anand Mohan, professor of religion at Queens College in New York, this practice was not voluntary.

Hindu gods in general represent heaven, light and fire, and demons represent darkness, chaos and the underworld. One can see the centrality of fire by looking at the Riq Veda, the oldest collection of hymns known to the Vedic Indians, from the second millenium B.C.E. There the god Agni represented fire. Agni is mentioned in over 200 hymns and is situated just below Indra, the number-one deity in the Hindu pantheon. Agni looks like fire: he has flaming hair, a golden beard, bright teeth and shining eyes, several tongues and he makes a crackling noise and leaves a smoky trail. Agni is constantly renewing himself, and is therefore both the oldest and the youngest god. Agni is the god of the priesthood and is intimately involved in sacrifice. His job is to ensure that the priests perform sacrifices correctly and to bring the burnt offerings to the other gods and, in return, bring the gods' blessing to the people.

Agni is a good example of how the Hindu concept of sacrifice has evolved over the millennia. Sacrifice still takes the form of material offerings and fire rituals but it has also become more abstract, more ethereal. The microcosmic fires inside a person's body are equated with the macrocosmic fires of the universe.

One can sacrifice one's self—through devotion, meditation and other forms of yogic asceticism, in an internal fire ritual that gives oneself over to Agni.

Agni is a male deity. But there were, and still are, female deities of fire and sun. Certain Siberians pray to the spirit, virgin or mother of fire. Scandinavian folk customs include a female fire deity. And Japan's Shintoism has its goddess Amaterasu, who represents light and purity. Amaterasu is the center of Shinto worship, and she is believed to be the ancestor of the first Japanese emperor. Another Shinto god, Susano-o-Mikoto represents earthly qualities. As one would expect from such a sophisticated society appreciative of great subtlety, light and darkness are complementary qualities and both are necessary to life.

THE SUN, ASCENDANT

The sun is so strongly identified with light as to be virtually inseparable from it. Although fire is the equivalent of sun on earth, religions often paid the celestial form separate homage, a practice that continues to influence religious cycles and holidays. For example, ancient Romans celebrated the Sol Invectus ("invincible sun"), a holiday that eventually became the date Christians celebrate Christmas.

The all-seeing, powerful, life-giving sun became the object of pagan adoration in many parts of the world. Ancient Greeks and Romans developed sun and sun bathing cults. Ancient Nordic cultures developed complex rituals for worshiping the rising sun— not surprising for a people who saw so little sun except during the summer, when it almost never sets. The sublimely mysterious Stonehenge also comes to mind. Ancient sun worshipers somehow positioned the gigantic stones, which recent carbon dating tells us are at least as old as the oldest pyramids, to mark the solstices and equinoxes (as well as the stations of the moon). On a smaller scale, archeologists have discovered many artifacts dating from this time—gold and bronze disks engraved with crosses, and gold-rimmed amber disks—nearby in Scotland, Brittany, the British Isles and Scandinavia. They appear to be amulets, reinforcing the probability of widespread sun worship. Northern Europeans still mark the summer solstice by lighting bonfires and rolling flaming wheels down hills, a custom that has likely not changed for thousands of years. Less directly, people still encourage the sun to return to its former glory during the winter solstice by burning the Yule log and the Chanukah candles.

Several highly developed ancient cultures are practically synonymous with major sun deities. Egypt of course is known for its long-lived adoration of the sun. In early Egypt, Horus was a falcon god and also representative of the sun and the sunrise.

Then came Re-Atum, around 2600 B.C., and the era of the first great pyramids built to face the sun. The Egyptians' exquisite art often depicted the sun sailing across the sky in a boat, sometimes accompanied by the pharaoh, who was his son or possibly just a good friend. Sometimes the sun is depicted as being swallowed by the Sky Mother and born again each morning from between her thighs. The pharaoh known as Amunhotep IV, or Akhenaton, tried to abolish worship of all other gods but Aton, the sun. He supported a new, naturalistic style of art, depicting him, his wife Nefertiti and his five daughters bathed in the brilliance of the sun, its rays in the form of tiny hands reaching down to caress them. This idea of worshiping only one god failed miserably. Akhenaton died mysteriously and a young man named Tut-Ankh-Amun (a.k.a. King Tut) seized power.

And what can one say about the sad progression of sun worship of the Maya, Toltec, Aztec and Inca people? The Mayans apparently developed a complex civilization with huge religious structures the size of a city. There, priests devoted time, energy and brainpower to studying mathematics (they invented the zero) and observing the sky. They had many deities, but the main one seems to have been a sky god and sun god, who was married to the moon.

The Mayan civilization mysteriously disappeared and was replaced by the Toltec from Central Mexico. The Toltec took sun worship one step further: they believed the Sun God died each night, but could be brought back to life each morning not with a great cup of coffee, but with human blood. Cannibalism was also on the menu and if the sacrificial lamb was a great warrior, pieces of him were distributed among the elite.

Next came the even less fathomable Aztecs, who took over the Toltec temples and made them sites of mass human sacrifice. Sometimes they offered up as many as 20,000 souls on their Pyramid of the Sun. Why a group of people felt they needed to go to such gruesome extremes in their religious practices is perhaps at least partly explained by the fact that they believed in the ongoing holy battle waged daily between light/life and darkness/death. They believed that there were five suns, four of which had been snuffed out by storms, floods and darkness. Only one, the one they lived under, remained but was in danger of being destroyed by earthquake. All of existence would cease to be if their sun, Tonatiuh, did not get fed every morning. Hence, their priests (possibly under the influence of psychedelic drugs), exhorted the Aztec armies into battle and took large numbers of prisoners to provide fodder for this bloodthirsty deity. It was overwhelming fear that drove them to sacrifice others to keep the rest of the world alive and well.

The Incas of Peru worshiped the Sun God, but in a somewhat less bloody form. There were huge festivals with processions, prayers, dances and sacrifices, usually of animals rather than humans. Of the four big yearly festivals, held on the solstices and equinoxes, the winter solstice was the most crucial. On this, their New Year's Day, all fires were relit, using a piece of cotton kindled by the rays of the sun, and then used in the sacrifices. Virgins of the

Sun were given the sacred duty of guarding the flames until the following year's celebration, when the process would be repeated.

Gold was the medium of worship and emulation. Since the sun symbolized royal power, gold images were everywhere. According to legend, the Inca tribe's founder and his sister were Children of the Sun. A golden wand was thrust down and into the Earth by the Sun, thereby determining the location of the Earth's first city. Each subsequent emperor (the emperor was thought to be the Son of the Sun) built his own palace, adding to the existing structures, eventually creating an elaborate maze of buildings generously decorated with gold. The Incas clearly believed more was better and lavished extravagant display and adornment of their gods and members of the royal family. They placed "sun columns" on the east and west hills outside the city, to mark the solstices. They clothed the mummies of emperors in gold and placed them and their wives around the temple of the Sun, and paraded them around the city on festivals. The temple, called the Place of Gold, contained a golden solar disk that filled the place with golden reflected sunlight at sunrise. When they died, Inca citizens who toed the line went to Sun's heaven along with the emperor and his "children of the sun."

Who knows what the Inca rituals would look like today, if they had survived? Perhaps they would have evolved from the bloody sacrificial events they were into something more positive and benign, as has the Sun Dance of the hunting tribes of the Great Plains of North America. The Sun Dance was a multi-purpose, weeklong, intense extravaganza that brought scattered peoples together mid-summer. Dances were performed to renew the earth, to bring fertility, to revenge a death. Although there were as many as thirty variations and interpretations depending on the tribe, a common element was to dance while gazing at the sun for a whole day, which must have caused a fair amount of pain. Another even more gruesome feature involved piercing the flesh of the breasts or shoulders and tethering the brave souls to a ceremonial altar as they danced until their flesh ripped.

These ceremonies were banned for some time by the US government, but were so much a part of the people's spiritual life that they were practiced in secret or modified forms. An enlightened attitude prevailed and today, the dances are practiced openly, but with greater attention to the spiritual aspect, not the torturous aspects common to the more military era. For example, the Shoshuni/Crow Sun Dance includes many rituals, but one is particularly beautiful. Every morning during the event, the dancers rise before sunup and assemble facing the rising sun. As they gently play eagle-bone whistles, they move slowly to the beat of a drum. As the sun ascends, the playing comes to a crescendo and the dancers extend eagle feathers toward the celestial ball of fire. They then touch the feather tips to parts of their body to receive the purifying blessings of the sun's first rays.

Today, except for the perennially bronzed George Hamilton, sun and light worship has pretty much fallen out of favor. It does survive in an indirect and disguised form in the celebration of holidays, and in the symbolic use of candles all year round.

BLESSED MOON AND SPARKLING STARS

The moon is a real problem in religion. It appears at night and thus is equated with darkness. But it can serve as a beacon and guide and symbol of hope during those witching hours. The moon changes more than any other visible heavenly body. The lunar pattern of waxing and waning, like the annual journey of the sun, echoes the very rhythms of life itself. The moon is smaller than the sun although it doesn't always appear so, and it's cool brightness is a mere reflection of the sun's rays.

Despite its diminutive and confusing status, the moon has subtle powers long recognized and honored, sometimes respected and often feared. The first known temple was a lunar temple, constructed about 2,800 B.C. Early peoples hailed the appearance of the new moon as a sign of its returning from the dead. The full moon was celebrated as a time of joy; the waning of the moon engendered anxiety. Lunar and solar eclipses inspired teeth-chattering terror. In more developed religions the moon is more complicated and even contradictory. It can be either male or female, kind or evil, capable of growth and fertility or of death and destruction. The cycles of the moon have long been recognized as being connected with female menstrual cycles and beneficent or disastrous tides and floods. In hot, topical and desert climates, the sun can be cruel and harsh; the moon therefore, becomes the good guy—or gal.

Mesopotamia—the land between the Tigris and Euphrates rivers—spawned the first urban civilization 7,000 years ago. The Sumerians of this civilization believed all gods were related. The creator Sky God is called An; his grandson Nanna was the Moon; his great grand children were Utu the Sun, and Ianna was the Evening Star. When the Assyrians replaced the Sumerians, they built their own moon city, Haran, on the Euphrates. Moonlight has always encouraged moonshine: in India of ancient times, men and gods drank *soma*, an intoxicating yellow-hued beverage identified with the yellow moon. There is a whole book of the Vedas dedicated to soma, a concoction made of a sacred plant. Soma was also a god, who dwelt in the heavens and banished the darkness.

Thanks to the lunar calendar, so common in so many cultures, the moon dictates the timing of many religious holidays and celebrations, including Passover and Christmas. The waxing and waning of the moon regulate Hindu festivals as well as marriages and other important events. According to Rachel McDermott, assistant professor of Asian and Middle Eastern culture, each month is divided into two halves—the "bright" half of the lunar month, and the "dark" half. "It has to do with the concept of auspiciousness and inauspiciousness," she says. "The brightest half, when the moon goes from dark to light, is an auspicious time, and that is when festivals and weddings generally occur. When the moon goes from light to dark, it is an inauspicious time, and that's when ancestor rituals are staged, because they are in the dark world of the dead."

Early Hebrews marked the arrival of the new moon with a family feast and animal sacrifice, with the months being named after the particular agricultural activity that took place. Muslims follow a lunar calendar, and each new month officially begins when two designated observers declare to the authorities that they have seen the new moon from either a mountaintop or an open field. The crescent moon shape (called a *hilal*) is emblematic in Islamic art.

The stars and other celestial bodies are a source of awe and wonder even today. Are they the home of our ancestors, of souls long dead, of souls waiting to be born? Do they watch over us protectively? Are they gods themselves? Is the polestar (North Star) the center of the Universe? Are comets and meteors omens of good or bad luck? Was the star of Bethlehem, which pointed the way to Christ's birth, a comet? Are comets the tails of the gods? Once they fall to earth are meteors sacred objects? Is the black rock imbedded in the Ka'bah of Mecca really a meteor brought to earth by the archangel Gabriel? All these celestial questions and more are part of the great rich tapestry of religion.

Today, the moon's main claim to fame seems to be its ability to rhyme with "croon" and "tune." As such, it is a romantic figure, made for encouraging midnight walks and ocean gazing. It has become a joke relegated to the realm of witches and sorcery, werewolves and insanity. Yet, there it is, every night, visible and invisible, creating a subtle somatic and soulful pull on all within its reach.

"I AM THE LIGHT"

Light and fire figure prominently and frequently in the Abrahamic religions, where light is the symbol of God's divine presence and also of personal salvation. For example, in the Hebrew Bible, we read, "The Lord is my light and my salvation" (Psalm 27); "In the light we shall see light" (Psalm 36); "Let us walk in the light of the Lord" (Isaiah 2); and God is "wrapped in a robe of light" (Psalm 104); "For the commandment is a lamp; and the law is light" (Proverbs 6:23); "The spirit of man is the candle of the Lord" (Proverbs 20:27); the Jewish people are "a light to the Gentiles" (Isaiah 40:6).

Lesli Ross writes, in her book, *Celebrate!: The Complete Jewish Holidays Handbook*, "All Jewish, and world, history is the struggle to maintain light against the force of darkness, a struggle between the sparks of creativity and the fires of destruction, between the shadow of evil and the radiance of human goodness, being in the dark of ignorance and seeing the light of truth."

In his book, *Hildegard of Bingen's Book of Divine Works*, Matthew Fox supplies these writings in which the notable nun of the Middle Ages equated fire with God when she put these words in God's mouth: "I, who am without beginning, am the fire by which all the stars are enkindled." And also, "I remain hidden in every kind of reality as fiery power. Everything burns because of me in such a way as our breath constantly moves us, like the wind-tossed flame in a fire. All lives in its essence and there is no death in it. For I am life." No wonder Quakers call God "The Divine Light Within."

Father Cormier points out that candlelight in particular is a hugely important symbol in Christian faith. "It moves, it looks and is alive, it gives life. It gives of itself without diminishing itself, just as you can give your faith and love without diminishing it. There is enough light for us all; in fact it increases when we share it." The Christian gospels extended the symbolism to God's son, Jesus, who dubbed himself the "light of the world," and claimed his followers would gain the "light of life." This has implications for both Christmas and Easter, as we shall see. Fire on the other hand, can be a manifestation of or an instrument of God—or a weapon of a wrathful God that inflicts purification, destruction, punishment and pain. The Bible burns with images such as "pillar of fire," "burning bush" and "chariot of fire," drawn by "horses of fire." And let us not forget the eternal fires of hell that unrepentant sinners will endure; nor the conflagration the New Testament proclaims will consume the world.

Back in today's world, the lighting of candles marks the beginning of the Jewish Sabbath. Rabbi Heschel writes in his book, *The Sabbath*:

> When all work is brought to a standstill, the candles are lit. Just as creation began with the word, "let there be light!" so does the celebration of creation begin with the kindling of lights. It is the woman who ushers in the joy and sets up the most exquisite symbol, light, to dominate the atmosphere of the home.

The light is the physical symbol and a reminder of God's eternal spiritual presence. The sun and stars determine the lighting of the candles and the beginning and end of the holy day. The candles are lit eighteen minutes before sunset to liberate an extra slice of time from the realm of imperfection, and then snuffed out forty-two or seventy-two minutes after sundown when the first stars are visible.

In mystical systems, light is almost synonymous with union with God. The ultimate goal of the mystic is to behold the pure light and beauty of the Creator. The Qur'an has its famous "light verses," and Islam has its own prophetic and metaphysical doctrine of light in which light began to be identified with the divine light principle. The Sufi poet Rumi calls God "the infinite open ray of light." In *The Illuminated Prayer*, Coleman Barks writes, "The moment Allah gazes upon this light, all the mysteries that had lain dormant burst from within him as rays of sparkling luminosity." The Holy Prophet said, "May divine light be before me, behind me, to the right and left, above and below. May my limbs be filled with divine light. May my skin be filled with divine light."

Even in Buddhism, which has no gods, light and fire are highly symbolic and used to describe the ineffable: reincarnation. Picture one lamp lighting another. "The second flame is distinct from the first, but it is burning as a result of the burning of the first flame. Nothing physical passes from one to the other, but the burning of the second depends upon the prior burning of the first," according to Mel Thompson in *Eastern Philosophy*. Cremation, death by fire and voluntary self-immolation are believed to aid the transition to immortality and transcendence, or at least rebirth to a higher existence in Hinduism and Buddhism. And then there is the word "enlightenment" itself— an English word, yes, but a noble attempt to describe the process of seeing things as they really are, which in turn leads to reunification with Brahman. Buddhism's practice of meditation is said to lead through innumerable spheres and worlds of light.

Rumi, who probably came closer to expressing the infinite with his poetry than any other human being, once said,

> Enough of phrases, conceit, and metaphors,
> I want burning, burning.

Rumi founded the whirling dervishes, who spin to kindle the physical and spiritual fire within, as does Gabrielle Roth, a dancer and author of *Sweat Your Prayers*. She writes:

> To sweat is to pray, to make an offering of your innermost self. Sweat is holy water, prayer beads, pearls of liquid that release your past, anointing all your parts in a baptism by fire. Sweat burns karma, purifying body and soul. Sweat is an ancient and universal form of self-healing, whether done in the gym, the

sauna, or the sweat lodge. I do it on the dance floor. The more you dance, the more you sweat. The more you sweat, the more you pray. The more you pray, the closer you come to ecstasy.

Dr. Anand, professor of Asian studies at the City University of New York, describes inner light this way: "Your body-mind complex is like an onion. The outermost layer, *anna-maya-kosha*, is the layer of "food" or the material body. The next is *prana-maya-kosha*, the "life force" or the bioenergetic field. *Mano-maya-kosha* is the "mind" or the lower mind that processes information from the senses. *Vijnana-maya-kosha* is "intelligence" or the higher mind of understanding and wisdom. Within this wisdom is *ananda-maya-kosha*, which is the true Self or the Ultimate Reality. The innermost layer is light; all the other layers are darkness."

Once one has become one with God, or at least seen Him or walked with Him, one glows. Jesus, Buddha, the saints and other divine figures are often depicted with halos surrounding their heads, auras surrounding their whole bodies or flames above their heads, making their divine transformation obvious for all to see. Visions are also often accompanied by light, often blinding light, as are alien abductions, this era's mystical equivalents.

SEASONS' GREETINGS

Look up. Is the sun at its highest point in the sky? If so, today is the brightest and longest day of the year. Still, this glorious celestial moment may be tinged with the realization that the day is also the pivotal point of a return to darkness. Think of it: this is the most sunlight you'll be seeing for the next 364 days. Tomorrow will be minutely shorter and one by one the days will begin to shorten and the nights will grow longer. It won't get any better than this. Isn't it time to light a fire and celebrate?

Look up again. Now the earth has spun half way around the

sun. The sun is at its lowest point in the sky. The days are short and the nights are long. It's the heaviest, darkest moment of the year. But still—the sun's wan appearance is tinged with hope and the promise that from now on, the days will get longer, we will progress steadily towards the warmth and light. It won't get any worse that this. That means it's time to light a fire and celebrate.

Time moves again. Now the days and nights are of equal length. It's time to plant the crops or time to harvest them. Time for the rains to begin or time for them to end. The moon is full or the moon is new. Any one of these times is another reason to celebrate. But do we take the time to mark these momentous occasions—do we even notice that they occur? Most of us live lives that no longer follow the path of the sun or pull of the moon. The strong distinct pulses of the seasons and the daily cycle have turned to mush. We can light up our nights and darken our days at will. We can eat mangoes while watching snow fall. Our lives are no longer centered on literal plantings and harvests, on sunrises and sunsets.

But these essential themes are still there, if you look hard enough. In many religions, these ideas have become metaphors: symbolic, poetic endings and beginnings, ways to stir the soul and give our lives a more beautiful shape. It's no accident that many of the most important religious holidays are seasonal celebrations—timed to coincide with the summer and winter solstices, the spring and autumn equinoxes, the cycles of the sun and moon. These seasonal underpinnings may be long buried under layers of history, but they are there—remnants of a time when people were all too aware of the rhythms of light and dark.

Chanukah, for instance, which is known as the Festival (or Feast) of Lights, takes place during the darkest days of winter. The winter solstice is a time of confusion and gloom. In response to this, Jews bring light into their lives, literally and symbolically. To the Jewish people, light represents knowledge and hope for a better future, a brighter life. The lesson of Chanukah is the incredible power of the spirit and the infinite ability of God's people to "live by the divine light," according to Irving Greenberg in *The Jewish Way*. The main symbol in the Chanukah celebration is the *menorah*, a nine-branched candelabrum symbolizing the light of God. Eight candles represent the eight nights of Chanukah; the ninth candle, which sits in the center, is the "servant" used to light the others. On the first night, the first candle is lit, on the second night, two candles, on the third night, three candles, and so on. Each night the family gathers together to light the menorah and recite or sing special blessings as they do so. "The progression moves us from faint illumination to darkness to light, from little hope in the present to faith in the future, an expression of expectations that our holiness, the impact we can have in the world, can and will increase," writes Lesli Ross in *Celebrate!: The Complete Jewish Holidays Handbook*.

Chanukah commemorates a miracle. First, a miracle of military might fueled by spirit: The Syrians wanted to obliterate Judaism so they vandalized the Temple in Jerusalem and forbade Jewish customs. But a small band of warriors, who came to be known as the Maccabees, successfully wrested the Holy Temple from the Syrians. However, the Temple had been sullied and they needed to purify and rededicate it—Chanukah means "dedication." As they prepared to rekindle the sacred eternal lamp, they discovered that there was only enough purified oil to last for one day. That's the second miracle, the miracle of the oil: according to legend, the tiny bit of oil miraculously burned for eight days—exactly the amount of time needed to obtain additional purified oil to keep the lamp lit. Hence, the eight candles and eight-day celebration involving many joyous customs and ceremonies.

Technically, Chanukah is a minor holiday in the Jewish calendar. It is not mentioned in the Jewish Bible, but it is the only important pre-modern festival for which there are definite historical records. Some say it has become popular and commercialized as a response to the overwhelming presence of Christmas, which falls around the same time of the year. But perhaps it is more than that—the strong symbolism of the light representing the perseverance of the Jewish spirit and distinct way of life despite tremendous pressures against them. Ross touchingly sketches the true spirit of Chanukah when she writes that "throughout the Holocaust, the Jews—saving bits of butter to fuel small flames held in hollowed potatoes—continued to thank God for the miracle of Chanukah, believing, as had the Jews under Rome, that another miracle was possible."

In India, most Hindu celebrations take place during the brightest time of the full moon. However, three festivals occur during the dark time of the moon—and one of these, Divali, is called the Festival of Lights. It is celebrated at the time of the autumn equinox, during the nights the moon makes the transition from its waning phase to its waxing phase. The equinox marks the end of the Indian rainy summer season and the beginning of the harvesting of the summer crops. The name Divali means "row of lights" and refers to the infinite number of oil lamps lit in each village in honor of the festival. The lamps serve to light the way for the ancestors and represent the hope kindled by the beginning of a new season and the survival of yet another time of monsoon. Along with the cacophonous display of firecrackers, the lights are meant to frighten the evil spirits and keep them away, while welcoming Lasksmi, the Hindu goddess of prosperity.

The festival lasts three nights, and in many ways is a rite of renewal and a New Year celebration. This is the annual opportunity for Hindus to settle their debts and merchants to settle their accounts. On the domestic front, Hindus cleanse and purify themselves and their homes. It is a time of offerings to Lashkmi—jewels, money, food and special clothes—and gifts to family and servants. Divali exemplifies the pragmatism and tolerance so characteristic of Hinduism, especially where wealth and prosperity are concerned. Hindus welcome and worship the demon king Bali, the demon Naraka and also Yama, the Lord of the Dead and king of the social and cosmic orders. The idea here is that order is restored when one is prosperous, and wealth and prosperity depend on the ancestors, women and demons of the underworld.

Christianity has a long and rich history of holidays related to the sun, moon and seasons, and Easter and Christmas are their glorious culmination, as James Fraser thoroughly shows in his classic book, *The Golden Bough*. Fire festivals, representative of our joy at harnessing one of nature's greatest forces, were popular in Europe, and originated in pagan times, way before Christianity was a twinkle in God's eye, but managed to trickle down through history and remain imbedded in rituals we perform today. Bonfires were most commonly lit in spring, but also in some regions at the end of autumn or midwinter. Gleeful villagers would dance around fires and leap over them, and sometimes burn an effigy of death. Belgians still light bonfires on the first Sunday of Lent, as do many French and Germans. Ritual bonfire celebrations can also still be observed in the Central Highland of Scotland, Wales, Ireland and other parts of Europe on the summer solstice, and in midsummer in Russia, Norway, Spain and Greece.

> And the desert shall rejoice, and blossom as the rose . . . then shall the lame man leap as an hart and the tongue of the dumb sing: for in the wilderness shall waters break out, and streams in the desert. And the parched ground shall become a pool and the thirsty land springs of water: In the habitation of dragons, where each lay, shall be grass with reeds and rushes.

What a miraculous transformation! This passage from the book of Isaiah is surely one of the most joyous, uplifting passages in the Bible. Could you tell that it is about spring, a time of rebirth and renewal, when the earth itself opens up and is ready to bring forth the plant life that has been sleeping inside her, and she is ready to receive new seed, new life?

Spring is Easter time, the time of Christianity's oldest and most sacred and joyous holiday because it celebrates the resurrection of Christ. After suffering the psychological and physical wounds of betrayal and crucifixion, Jesus lay in his cave tomb for three days of the dark moon, the equivalent of winter, when life sleeps. With his resurrection, came the miracle of rebirth, bringing with him light, life and salvation.

Unlike Christmas, Easter is a moveable feast, and is fixed to fall on the first Sunday following the first full moon after the spring equinox. Easter comes from Eoster, the name of the Anglo Saxon goddess who brought the dawn of each day, as well as the dawn of each New Year. The resurrection took place during Passover, and initially the Eastern Church celebrated both Passover and Easter. "Light represents Christ and darkness is the absence of light, of God; we see this most clearly and dramatically during the great vigil of Easter" says Frank Tedeschi, managing editor of Church Publications Co. One can't help but be swayed after listening to him describe the vigil service at St. Luke In The Field, the Episcopal church he attends in Lower Manhattan.

The liturgy begins in total darkness, "symbolizing that with Jesus' death and burial on Good Friday, something had left the world," says Tedeschi. Imagine: the church is pitch black. "Then a large candle called the paschal candle is lit. The deacon or another cleric walks down the aisle with the candle, pausing three times, singing 'the light of Christ, thanks be to God,' each time. He uses the flame to ignite the candles held by the assembly, until the whole church is aglow with the candlelight, symbolizing the carrying of the light of Christ into the world, which is every Christian's responsibility." In Tedeschi's church the vigil begins at 8 p.m. In ancient tradition, the vigil began in the middle of the night and ended at dawn, a tradition that some churches are trying to bring back. People stayed in the church all night, keeping the vigil in silence, prayer and song.

If the structure of this Easter service sounds suspiciously like the elements of the Plymouth Church of the Pilgrims Advent service described in chapter one, that's because they are. Christmas and Easter are the highest points of the Christian liturgical year, ritual observances that are "the purest form of the love of God in the Christian faith," says Reverend Blackburn of the Plymouth Church. Both holidays embody the progression from dark to light, although they fall at opposite times of the year. In each holiday, says Blackburn, "darkness represents the lack of salvation or waiting for the hope of salvation. Then the light of Jesus comes and shows us the path to salvation."

The Advent season—four weeks of reflection and preparation for the big day of Jesus' birth—ushers in Christmas day. Although the world may be dark and bleak, Advent is a time for hope, rejoicing, waiting and expectancy. A hopeful longing for the return of the sun mirrors the Christian longing and preparation for the coming of Christ. Finally, after a month of preparation, patience is rewarded. Accompanied by feelings of joy and exuberance, the world is transformed by Christ's light. Jesus is the light of the world, and his saving grace is within everyone's reach, as is written in Luke: "Behold, I bring you good tidings of great joy, which shall be to all people, for unto you is born this day in the City of David, a savior, which is Christ the Lord." Like Chanukah, Christmas is celebrated with candles and lights. Beginning with the star of Bethlehem announcing Christ's birth 2,000 years ago, to the twinkling lights on Christmas trees, Christmas is a bright pool of light in the middle of winter's deep shadow.

It is a yearly reminder that amidst the darkness of life, when it is darkest of all, when it can't get any darker, at that moment you turn the corner and feel the beginning of the light. It is a reminder of the light within us, says Reverend Blackburn, and that we can transform the world with our light. In a Christmas sermon, she says, "Christ will baptize you with the Holy Spirit and fire. He will strengthen and empower you, make you a partner, using all the potential created within you, in the building of God's Kingdom on earth."

Yet for all their brightness, the dancing flames and colorful twinkling lights serve also to blind us to the underlying meaning of this winter holiday. It's not just the longer nights that darken the soul. All the hoopla only heightens the restless longing for what we don't have. Media and merchants alike parade before us not only us the possibilities of love, compassion, sacrifice, giving, sharing, family, warmth and God, they also peddle their warehouses of merchandise and besotted office and other parties. Are these reminders or distractions from the celebration of the true spirit of Christmas? Despite the ads and the special sales, Christmas is not about gifts; it is about giving, and about sharing with others what little light we have.

SEEING THE LIGHT—AND THE DARK

Physical light—the sun, candles, electric menorahs—is the metaphor for the invisible light that is the essence of God and permeates all creation. But can physical light actually lead to enlightenment? Can it affect the light within us? Religion says, Yes.

All through history, sunlight and color were used as medical therapy, as part of a people's worldview and to enhance spirituality. In fact, this approach may have been one of the first forms of medicine. The Egyptians, Assyrians and Babylonians all practiced therapeutic sunbathing. Also, color therapy was used to heal mind and body. The preferred technique was to lead patients into special rooms, each of which had windows covered with a different color cloth, which bathed the room and the patient in light of a particular color, depending on the ailment. Today, the stained glass windows of the cathedrals of the world exhibit a similar effect in their ability to inspire and lift the spirit.

In some cultures and belief systems moonlight is considered to be therapeutic. In India, Muslims fill a silver vessel with water set it in the moonlight, and then drink the water in a practice called "drinking the moon." Hindus also use moonlight as therapy, and believe that exposing the skin to the moon's cool light—either from a moonlight stroll or sitting or lying near an open window—during the full moon, calms an overheated disposition.

Once again, science and medicine are catching up with traditional practices and discovering the tantalizing possibility that light can have profound effects on the body, mind and spirit. Literally and metaphorically you are what you "eat." Light and dark significantly effect every cell and regulating system of the body—the hormone system, immune system and nervous system—which in turn influence all the other systems and organs.

Scientists are busy studying light and colors (the components of light) and beginning to use them to treat an amazing spectrum of ailments of the body, mind and soul. These include deficiencies in the production, absorption and utilization of nutrients including vitamin D and calcium and the production of the hormone melatonin, which affects our 24-hour body rhythms, immune system and moods. Melatonin irregularities are linked with irritability, fatigue, insomnia, menstrual problems, jet lag, depression and suicide. Lack of sunlight has in particular been linked with winter depression, or seasonal affective disorder (SAD).

This suggests, among other things, that not all light is created equal. Our light bulbs give us 24-hour light, but the light they emit is artificial. *In Light Years Ahead*, Dr. Brian Breiling writes:

> Sunlight is one of the most pleasurable, joyful, energizing, and omnipresent blessings in our lives. The radiant energy of the sun is the major source of vitality and power for every organism

on the planet. Our species has evolved and thrived under the entire color spectrum of natural sunlight, thus, we are genetically programmed to respond to these specific frequencies of light. Yet, since the Industrial Revolution we have moved our activities inside which creates working and living conditions that keep us away from this life giving source of energy.

Amen.

George Brainard, who investigates light's medical uses, believes that our indoor lighting generally doesn't fulfill our biological requirements since it is of a level that is equivalent to natural outdoor light at 5 p.m. We spend much of our time in a kind of "twilight zone." Tinted windows, glasses and contact lenses also filter out important components of light, compounding the problem, since our eyes are an important gateway for light's biological effects. But it is the skin where sunlight stimulates production of vitamin D. It may also be through the skin that light helps us set our biological clocks each day, which in turn regulates our physiology, our behavior and mood.

Furthermore, artificial light lacks the full range of color and intensity of sunlight. Since we spend ninety percent of our time indoors, we are left light starved to varying degrees all year round. Insufficient light and exposure to harmful light and electromagnetic radiation from computer screens can lead to eyestrain, headache and blood problems, according to Dr. John Ott, a pioneer in light research. Full spectrum light (that is, light from the sun or specially designed light bulbs), on the other hand, seems to increase productivity, improve thinking, benefit the immune system and decrease on-the-job accidents and absenteeism. Full-spectrum lighting has also affected students' academic ability, physical growth and over all health and vitality, according to Canadian psychologist Dr. Warren Hathaway. With such a pathetic exposure to natural light, no wonder we find it such a challenge to achieve enlightenment.

Although it is tempting to do so, light and dark cannot be reduced to good and bad. For every glimpse we get of divine light and consciousness, we must also remember and honor what is dark and messy about life. These are complementary aspects in life that we need to recognize and balance. We need to engage and embrace the whole of reality. It's easy to love the lighter side of life and of God. But darkness reveals the light by its contrast—in a sense, without darkness, there would be no light. Both are part of the human experience.

Rabbi Bronstein of B'nai Jeshurun in New York City says,

We are grateful to be able to go from light to darkness. Darkness and night represent in the mystic tradition a type of twilight zone. It's a moment when you are closer to the divine, a moment when the boundaries are lost between life and death. This is the time the mystics would study because darkness gives you the ability to approach the deepest level of understanding of reality and of the text that you are studying. We also have certain services that begin at midnight, when we are tired, not completely awake, and there is a sense of mystery.

We and other living creatures need the rest that darkness provides. If we were always awake and intensely active, we would soon expire of exhaustion. In fact, many studies show that our ability to extend the daytime via artificial light is also hazardous to our health. Overexposure to even the comparatively weak nighttime light of civilization has been linked with sleep disturbances, hormone disruption, immune system irregularities and even increased risk of breast cancer. Late night TV, reading, even street lamps shining through our bedroom windows seem to be exerting an unacknowledged and subtle but real effect on us.

The Eastern philosophies seem to understand the balance best.

The next time you see a Chinese landscape painting, look closely. Notice how the artist depicts the shapes, the distance, the texture, the movement of trees, water, birds, clouds, mountains. Such paintings eloquently and wordlessly express the heart and soul of the Chinese philosophy of Tao, which means "the way, or the way of nature." As you gaze at the painting, think about the Tao—how all things come into being out of darkness; and how they move out of the light and return to darkness. These two principles of light and dark rhythmically interact and form all the shades in between in an endless flickering that comprises "the world of ten thousand things."

Perhaps at this point in our evolution, we need to be careful of being greedy—greedy for light, for enlightenment, for God— before we are capable of truly understanding these things. We have marvelous technology, but because of our immaturity, we are a danger to ourselves. Look what happened when we learned how to split the atom. It was too much power, too much uncontrolled light in the form of ionizing radiation, and now the world is poisoned. Reverend Blackburn muses, "The light of Christ is not some beaming individual. Rather, it is light in the sense of enabling us to see, if even for a glimpse, visions of love. It is that illumination, even if it is temporary and fleeting in a moment of childlike innocence, that allows us to realize something well beyond us. It is too much for mere mortals to hold."

This is why the temples in India are pitch dark. Professor Mohan describes the scene:

> You cannot see anything, representing that the world is dark. Then you go and you pray that you may see the light. The priest performs all these rituals that you cannot see. Then at the very end, he puts a little bit of camphor near the deity. He lights it. And for a trice of time in a second, he shows the face of the deity. Then it's gone. Very dramatic! That instant is the instant of illumination. All that you need in this life is that instant. All we get is a glimpse—and catching that glimpse is enlightenment.

5. *Feasting and Fasting*

The more you eat, the less flavor;
the less you eat, the more flavor.
—Chinese Proverb

Whispers and odours and the
tantalizing noises of banqueting
floated swiftly westward.
—M.F.K. Fisher, *The Art of Eating*

Family and friends sit around a table set with dazzling white napkins and old, polished silver that has been in the family for longer than anyone can remember. Ritual dishes of chopped apples and nuts, hard-boiled egg with parsley, a gnarled and bitter horseradish root adorn the table. Starched linen covers matzohs, the flat bread of oppression. The door to the house is open and a solitary glass of wine sits on the middle of the table, awaiting the arrival of the angel Elijah, who has yet to come but heralds the Coming of the Messiah.

As you sit around the table, empty plates and glasses gleam, taunting you with their bareness, teasing you with the foreknowledge of the plenitude to come. The reading of the *Haggadah* begins, the Passover story, retelling of the Exodus everyone has heard every year since birth, and which is a great source of inspiration, learning and understanding for participants—but that everyone still flubs when it's his or her turn to read! Of course you stumble—you're faint from hunger, delirious with anticipation. Finally, you arrive at the moment of partaking of the ritual foods, their significance woven into the story. The sips of sweet purple wine go straight to your head. Although you've been eating matzohs for weeks, at the breaking of the Passover matzoh, you realize no pot roast, no noodle pudding, no lox and bagel ever looked so good as this dry, tasteless cracker. You can't blame Grandpa for breaking ranks and pretending that his mouth is not filled with matzoh, telltale crumbs falling on his chest. "Grandpa!" This, too, is part of the ritual feast.

Finally, it's time to eat the tiny bites of tiny portions, at the appointed times, just the sensation of taste to fulfill the story. As always, the first crunch elicits a gush of digestive saliva that is so urgent, it's painful. The egg, the herb, the apple, the songs; the story continues to unfold. You can feel the eyes of everyone scanning the dishes, searching for miniscule bits of sustenance, but everything has disappeared, even the horseradish. Finally, the story is over, Israel is delivered from slavery and huge bowls and platters of matzoh ball soup, potatoes, meats, vegetables, kugels and desserts finally emerge from their hiding place, waiting to be overeaten, to play their parts in the fullness of Passover.

Ah, Passover. The only holiday where it can be said that you fast and feast at the same time.

What could be more basic to life than food and more gut-wrenching than the lack of it? We love to eat, beginning with mother's milk—and possibly even before that, since fetuses appear to ingest small amounts of amniotic fluid while still in the womb. We love the millions of subtle tastes and textures on our tongue, the tantalizing aromas, the eye-dazzling colors, the arrangement of grapes on a plate. We love the feel of a full belly. We love God for bestowing us with this soul- and body-satisfying gift. Food is joy and food is pleasure. Food is sustenance. Food is life. And food is part of the warp and weft of our cultures. So it's not hard to understand that our religions are also bound up with food, that God and holidays should be involved in our feasting, that food should also nurture our souls. But then, does it make sense that our religions tell us to also do the opposite—to fast, to deny ourselves of one of life's greatest pleasures and crucial necessities? Oh, yes.

Food is real, as real as it gets; but it is also highly symbolic. The withholding of food is also hugely symbolic, and most rituals and feasting holidays also have an element of denial and sacrifice. Sometimes fasting can be as hugely satisfying as indulging in a full meal.

DAYS OF FEASTING AND DAYS OF FASTING

What's a Sabbath, a Sunday, a zikr, a birth, a wedding, a funeral or any holiday without its big communal meal? We celebrate with food, and the original feasts and festivals were sacred communal meals that celebrated food itself with food. These ancient holidays were usually tied to the agricultural cycle or the seasons, which determined whether a people would live or die of starvation, and planting and harvest time were particular occasions for rejoicing. Festivals usually culminated or kicked off with a big party that included special foods and plenty of them.

This was an era when the food supply was extremely precarious, synonymous with the earth, dependent on rainfall and sunshine and the favor of the gods. It was a time when people lived from paycheck to paycheck and almost the entire paycheck consisted of edibles. So, all was not fun, games and gluttony. A price had to be paid to ensure prosperity and these festivals were often preceded by a period of fasting, which was often accompanied by other abstentions and trials. To please the gods, our forebears stopped eating so that they might eat, and survive, and that we might be here perhaps carrying on the tradition in some fashion. If we are even slightly observant, we do carry on the tradition although the rationale might seem obscure.

Today, the major religions incorporate into major holidays the rhythm of feasting and fasting as remnants of these agricultural holidays; for example, the springtime period of Lent that precedes Easter in Christianity, the autumnal Yom Kippur for the Jewish people and the moveable month of Ramadan in Islam. But for some this practice is more central than others.

Yom Kippur is the last day of the Jewish New Year or Rosh Hashanah. It was originally a harvest holiday called Hagha-Asif, or "feast of gathering." The culmination of ten days of introspection, taking stock and spiritual renewal, Yom Kippur is also called the "day of purification." This is the big opportunity to atone for one's sins and ask forgiveness for one's failings. It is based on the Bible passage "For on this day, you shall practice denial and self control." Jews are required to take no food or drink for twenty-five hours and express self-denial by not wearing leather goods, refraining from bathing oils, make up, perfumes and sexual relations.

Early Christians ate no food on Fridays to commemorate the death of Jesus Christ. Later, the forty days before Easter, called Lent, were also set aside as fasting days. "The idea of fasting and withdrawing is based on the model of Jesus," says Frank Tedeschi, managing editor of the Church Publishing Company, "because He spent forty days and forty nights fasting in the wilderness, being tempted by the devil." During this time Christians are supposed to meditate on Jesus' sufferings. Other fasting times were Rogation Days in spring to ask for good crops, and Ember Days during each of the four seasons.

Now the Roman Catholic Church requires only two days of fasting per year: Ash Wednesday and Good Friday. Catholics are allowed one full meal a day, plus two smaller meals that do not add up to a full meal. In Eastern Orthodox Christianity, the strict or orthodox are expected to fast a few additional days. But the "strictest" rules of "fasting" only require abstaining from meat, fish, wine, oil and dairy products. In the Protestant Church, fasting is optimal and left up to the individual. Today, Protestants usually give up a specific favorite food or activity for Lent. You call that fasting?

Obviously, neither Jews nor their Christian brethren seem terribly enamored of the fasting part of this rhythm. The following food-centric Jewish folk saying, as related by Irving Greenberg in *The Jewish Way: Living the Holidays*, pretty much sums it up. "Shavuot is the best among the holidays because one can eat whatever one likes, wherever one likes, and whenever one likes—as opposed to Pesach when chametz (leavening) is prohibited; Sukkot when meals are to be taken only in the sukkah; Rosh Hashanah when you can eat only after completing the lengthy prayers; and Yom Kippur when you may eat not at all."

For true fasting as a major beat in the rhythm of contemporary religious life, we must turn to Islam, which devotes the entire month of Ramadan to fasting. Fasting is one of the "five pillars" of Islam—it is a holy obligation and a commandment from God. The Arabic word for this fast is *sawm*, meaning to "refrain." Muslims not only refrain from food and drink but from sexual activity and all forms of immoral behavior, such as false words, deeds and intentions. The fast begins at first light, when the "white thread of light becomes distinguishable from the dark thread of night at dawn," and similarly ends at last light.

Ramadan is a time of introspection and private and communal prayer. It recalls the receiving of the Qur'an by Muhammad.

Muslims who fast and pray are forgiven their sins. In some Muslim communities businesses reduce work hours, since Muslims are hungry, tired and dehydrated during most waking hours. When Ramadan falls during the long hot days of summer, many officials and businessmen leave for Europe. Muslims may also fast on Mondays and Thursdays, and of course during certain days of the *hajj*, or pilgrimage to Mecca.

Fasting is also an important part of the rhythm of a Hindu's life. Dr. Anand Mohan, professor of Asian studies at City University of New York, says that according to Hindu philosophy, "you need to give your body a rest, so you adopt a fast one day a week. For example, certain days are earmarked for certain gods and goddesses. If you are a worshiper of Shiva, you will fast on a Monday." As is typical of this most holistic of all traditions, what's good for the body is also good for the spirit. Hinduism is rich with elaborate soul-satisfying myths and beliefs about the deities and their escapades, many of which provide the rationale for contemporary practices. For example, Hindus observe an annual fasting day called Shiva-rathis in honor of a legendary struggle between the gods and the demons over a pot of delicious nectar. As Mohan tells the story:

A snake is attached to the nectar, and the gods and demons are in a tug of war pulling on the snake. So the snake comes close to spurting out all its venom—enough to destroy the world. Shiva saves the human race by swallowing all the venom and holding it in his Adam's apple. So, to celebrate that Shiva saved us all, on this day Hindus fast, and all night we remain awake, plunged into darkness and sorrow, just as Shiva could not rest as long as he had the poison. The next morning we go to the temple and partake of food that has been offered to Shiva to receive his grace.

In some traditions, a period of feasting precedes the period of fasting. This symbolically celebrates life's excesses before the period of austerity. In many Roman Catholic countries the time before Lent is known as *carnival*—a word probably derived from *carne vale*, which in Latin means "farewell, meat"—a reference to the now outmoded custom of refraining from eating meat during Lent.

The most flamboyant example of this is Mardi Gras or "Fat Tuesday." Technically the Tuesday preceding the Christian period of Lent, Mardi Gras is now a more prolonged period of festivities. The most famous Mardi Gras is in New Orleans, Louisiana. Millions of tourists join the locals in their two-week-long, over-the-top celebrations, which include parades, pageants, masked balls, scantily clad women and lots of local food and drink. To not eat too much appears to be a sin in this instance: the "Gras" in Mardi Gras refers to the custom of consuming all the fats in the house before Lent begins.

Yom Kippur also begins with a hearty, festive meal or day of feasting, because as Matthew Fox observes, "it has to last us a long time." Yom Kippur is broken with only a light meal, but "we feast on the richness and splendor of forgiveness and renewal" that are the themes of the holiday, says Fox. During the twenty-nine days of fasting during Ramadan, Muslims compensate with pre-dawn breakfast feasts and festive nighttime meals. The nighttime *iftar* is a prolonged affair during which Muslims reward their daylong abstention with dates, apricots, sweetened milk and proceeds through many courses of vegetables, breads and meat. Friends and relatives visit each other and children race, singing through the streets. Ramadan ends with *Eid al-Fitr*, a big party with lots of special foods, gifts and prayers that last up to four days, a time of sweet exuberant relief from the hardship they have just endured.

Easter, says Frank Tedeschi, is "the greatest feast in the

Christian year. Feasting on a great meal is a way of giving thanks—we celebrate that there is something beyond death." Such feasting-and-fasting holidays are meant to give us a new lease on life. The original significance of literally renewing life from year to year and of having enough to eat resonates down through the centuries as a spiritual renewal. These holidays were often the beginning of "the New Year," and once the old and impure were eliminated, there was a period of reinvigoration to stimulate crop growth and encourage the rebirth of the land. This took the form of a ritual combat performance between Fertility and Blight, or of sanctioning sexual license (the rape of the Sabine women may reflect this custom), or enacting a sacred marriage of the gods. The offspring of this marriage symbolized new life and gave birth to the image of the baby in today's New Year's cards and festivities. In Fasching, the Lenten ceremony of Bavaria, sexual licentiousness is still practiced and spouse swapping is supposedly common.

OF TOFU AND TABOOS

It seems the traditions that encourage people to enjoy food the most fully also tend to have the strongest taboos relating to food. To say that Jewish people seem to have a unique relationship with food would be an understatement of several orders of magnitude. Food, food, glorious food is interwoven with the religion and especially their history as a people, as well as their emotion-layered personal history.

Like so much of Judaism, food is an issue laced with tears and fears, joys and memories. Leon Klenicki, a rabbi with the Anti-Defamation League says that "because of our deprivation during the Holocaust and before," food took on an import of gargantuan proportions. "I can remember my mother pushing food at me—she would say, 'Children are starving in Europe, you should be grateful and enjoy, you never know when you are going to eat again.'" A refrain that echoes in the memories of an entire generation, Jewish or not.

Claudia Roden, in her book, *The Book of Jewish Food* writes, "Every cuisine tells a story. Jewish food tells the story of an uprooted, migrating people and their vanished worlds. It lives in people's minds and has been kept alive because of what it evokes and represents." In *Wise Words*, Jessica Gribetz writes, "The dishes we prepare and share celebrate our roots and symbolize continuity. Each time I roll the pastry dough for mandebrot, I am somehow in the company of Grandma Martha, dipping her hand into the canister for just a bit more flour."

Many individual foods also have specific symbolic meaning in the Jewish tradition. During the eight days of Passover, Jews eat only unleavened bread (matzoh) to symbolize the haste with which the Jewish slaves fled from Egypt. During the Passover seder, they eat symbolic foods: a roasted egg symbolizes an offering and the continuity of life; a green vegetable represents renewal and is dipped in saltwater to symbolize the sweat and tears of Jews ancestors' slavery in Egypt; a bitter herb such as horseradish is a reminder of the horror of slavery; and charoset, a mixture made of chopped apples, nuts and wine symbolizes the mortar the slaves used to make the bricks used for pyramids. During the festival of weeks or Shavuot, which originated as a harvest celebration, families have festive meals which include wine and dairy products as a symbol of the "milk and honey" that is the Torah. Potato latkes, pancakes fried in oil, commemorate the miracle of the oil at Chanukah.

Strict Jews also follow food restrictions all year round. The restrictions are called *kashrut* and food is either kosher or nonkosher. All vegetables are allowed, but meats are limited—no pork or shellfish for example, and animals must be slaughtered according to certain dietary laws. In addition, milk and meat cannot be eaten or cooked together. Wine is sacred and is blessed during certain rituals. Islam's rules also prohibit pork, and other animals that have been improperly slaughtered, as well as alcohol. Christianity generally does not have any dietary restrictions, but some denominations forbid drinking alcohol or caffeine, or stimulants of any kind.

Buddhists are generally vegetarians because it is believed that it is compassionate not to kill animals, and are encouraged to eat locally grown foods in season. Some lay Buddhists emulate Buddhist monks and take only one bowl of food per day at certain times. But Buddhism generally takes a pragmatic and relaxed attitude toward food. So, even if you are invited to dinner and they are serving roast beef, says Kobutsu, you eat it. "It's polite, and not eating it will not bring the cow back." Many Buddhists believe the renunciation of wrong ideas is a better road to enlightenment than food fetishes. Kobutsu adds, "Some people fast as a form of purification, or self denial, or some damn thing. I grew up in the Bronx, so I always take a full bowl and pass on the tofu."

Hindus love food and feel you should enjoy it. Yet they have a rather elaborate system of dietary customs, beliefs and categorization based on notions of purity and contamination, health, the caste system, economics as well as religion. Food has many properties and they all figure into meal planning because the body is the temple of the divine and must be fed the proper food in the proper amounts and proportions at the proper time. For example, they divide food into three basic categories. Of these, *sattvic* foods—fruits, vegetables, and grains and nuts—are the most desirable because they are light and produce good physical, mental, and spiritual health and thus are good for preparing yourself for meditation.

Vegetarianism is the most desirable way of eating, but those who eat flesh still avoid beef because cows are sacred, and pork because pigs are unclean. In addition, says Mohan, "Food has five tastes—sweet, sour, salty, pungent and bitter. You need to have all five tastes in a meal, because your body needs them." He continues, "All the pleasures of the body are sacred and divine. You should enjoy good food, but eat according to dharma. Don't overeat or you will get indigestion, and that is stupid! You owe something to your body—you do not overload it. Feast, and enjoy, but you need to be moderate and observe your limits."

LESS IS MORE, RELIGIOUSLY

It's obvious why we feast: to partake and celebrate Nature's bounty to the fullest, to enjoy the company and fellowship of our friends, family and communities, to let go and eat with abandon. But what do we gain by giving up food for God?

In ancient religions, people made an offering of life-sustaining food to the deity or deities, as a symbol of their gratitude for the god's beneficence. Giving up food is a form of sacrifice—what you give to the deities you cannot yourself eat. So, giving food back to the deity was a major ritual in ancient religions. The most valuable offering was either "first fruits"—the first fresh, tender, succulent and long-awaited vegetable, grains or fruits harvested; or the first kill or first born of a domesticated animal. Animal sacrifice may sound horrible to us today (just as eating meat is barbaric to vegetarians) but it was a logical offering in ancient times.

For most of history, meat was not an everyday food—it was a rare occurrence and hence a very valuable and fitting gift to the gods. Animal sacrifice was a well-established practice in Judaism, with the Scriptures providing instructions for sacrifice that were typical of the era. In those days the community participated in killing and or raising the animal, preparing it and then feasting on what was left over after offering the choicest bits to the gods. Thus, this practice was the ultimate act of community, and enabled people to bond with each other and then as a unified body to identify with the deity.

In Hinduism, the gods still get fed regularly—temple services are lengthy, elaborate affairs where the image of the deity is bathed and then showered with oil, milk, yogurt or buttermilk, ghee (clarified butter, a symbol of purity), honey and brown sugar, according to Dr. Mohan. This is part of a sixteen-step ritual that is designed to "make the deity fed like an honored guest" in your temple or house. "Food is Brahman," declares Mohan. "Everything we receive from Him is Him. That's why we make offerings of food. If you cannot afford food, you offer yourself—your time, your energy. You pray, you meditate, you circumambulate the temple."

Since being hungry is an unpleasant hardship, it has a long consistent history as a means of purification and penance. The ancient Egyptians, Jews, Christians, Muslims and others have undertaken fasting to cleanse themselves of wrongdoing, to purify the spirit and to rid the body of its attachment to physical comforts and pleasures.

Fasting was a predominant feature in Christianity, particularly during the Middle Ages. Along with other ascetic practices, it was a way to deal with the tension between the body (which is earthy) and the soul (which is divine). Excessive fasting became so popular that monks had to be warned against it. In some circles, fasting was a way to exorcise demons, summon God's mercy and purge the person of temptations of the flesh and the world— a potent weapon against the contamination of sin. Among some Native American tribes, fasting was a crucial prerequisite for hunting and combat because prolonged fasting and praying purified and strengthened the body.

Communal fasting often includes a collective confession of sins. There is an element of forgiveness in Ramadan, but Yom Kippur takes the repentance cake. In this New Year ritual, fasting is a form of purification—it ritualistically removes noxious elements and the impurity of sins committed that year. In ancient times the Temple sanctuary and its vessels were also purified. What about sins that remained hidden and unpurged? No problem. The Israelites, like other peoples, symbolically removed latent, unconfessed sins by loading them on a scapegoat (animal or human) and then driving it away from the community.

Fasting also has a long history as a preparation for divine revelation or communication with the Divine. It was commonly practiced for this purpose in the Greco-Roman mystery religions, and shamans often use fasting to produce visions. Hebrew prophets fasted to produce trancelike states through which revelations could occur, so did the Sufis. Hindu ascetics fasted while on pilgrimage and to enhance meditation; they believed prolonged fasting helped accumulate *tapas* (heat), which eventually became supernatural powers. Many Native American tribes believed that fasting helped them receive guidance from the Great Spirit, and this was part of the ritual wilderness quest undertaken by a young brave to put him in touch with his guardian spirit.

Religious fasting can have a wide-reaching ripple effect and stimulate reflection and growth in many areas of our lives. A true fast frees up an astounding amount of time and energy you usually spend planning, buying, preparing, eating and washing up, allowing you to focus on spiritual matters such as praying or meditating. In purifying your body, you also think about purifying your mind and your life in general. Fasting becomes a time to take stock, to evaluate, to prioritize. As Matthew Fox writes of Yom Kippur, praying with an empty stomach allows you to focus completely, to examine the depth of your soul. Furthermore, wiping the slate clean and making amends with each other during the holiday, he says, fosters open communications, intimacy and resolution.

Advocates of fasting for religious purposes say it teaches self-responsibility, discipline and control of earthly appetites and passions. It also conditions you to be strong enough to resist temptations and laziness at other times in life. Fasting is a test: it gives you a sense of the extent to which you can control yourself and your appetites. If you can successfully resist your hunger for food, perhaps you can also resist your hunger for other things you thought you couldn't do without—such as material objects, power or control over others.

Many people find that following their religion's general dietary restrictions, day in and day out, to be more of a challenge than following a strict fast for a finite period of time. As is the case in watching your weight, it is easier to change your eating behavior dramatically for a short time than to stay on a maintenance diet the rest of your life. In recognition of this reality, Herman Wouk writes in *This Is My God*, "It is one of the sore points where observance tends first to break down . . . The non-observant dig in their heels at the whole idea. The devout, on the other hand, who have to work pretty hard at keeping up the diet, expect to be praised, and they want the nonobservant excoriated . . . we are looking at a detail of a symbol system that stamps all the customary acts of life . . . an act that all people perform several times a day, given the choice." A tough line to toe in the real world of McEverything.

To make such restrictions easier to swallow, some people cite medical or hygienic grounds as a rationale. Such efforts to justify most eating taboos have been spectacularly unsuccessful. No matter. In *Living Judaism*, Dosick argues that we don't need a reason. The only reason we have and the only one we need is: "Because God said so." He explains, "Obeying a law of God—especially without knowing the rationale behind the law—helps develop a sense of discipline and self control." Like true fasting, it is an ability that can carry over into other parts of your life. Having said no to delicious smelling pork chops (or any food, during a fast), even though you are famished, helps you develop the skills you need when facing an ethical dilemma. Even though you desperately

need money, you do not steal; even though you are greatly attract-
ed to that married woman, you do not seduce her. "Kashrut is less
about eating than it is about behaving," Dosick believes. It is "hal-
lowed through the centuries and is a uniquely defining characteristic of Jewish life," a life that strives to be ethical and moral.

The rhythm of periodically feasting and fasting expresses the
underlying life principle of plenitude and scarcity and teaches us to
live with this dynamic. Doing without sharpens your appreciation
of food and lets you thank God sincerely and with more awareness
of food and life itself. All religions include saying a blessing or giving thanks but we can easily forget to take a moment to do this in
the busyness of modern life. We need a reminder to appreciate
what we have. Just as the Sabbath helps us reshape time, food
restrictions "reshape the eating experience," writes Greenberg in
The Jewish Way. They place "a homogenized biological act" within "a grid of value and meaning, much as a gourmet seeks to
heighten the eating experience through selection, preparation and
rituals of eating."

"Feasting and fasting reinforce the idea of the cycles of nature,
and the ups and downs, prosperity and adversity—yes, they are all
there. You can be under the false illusion that any prosperity you
are enjoying is permanent," says Mohan. "So once a year as small
children, our heads were shaved and we were given a begging bowl
and had to obey so the idea of adversity extended our conscience."

Similarly, Reverend Sharon Blackburn says that there is a sense
in the Christian tradition that you are giving up something for
Lent. "But you are also taking something on; you take on a task
that helps you think of the meaning of this time of year. In the
Christian faith, one is asked to become fully whole so we can give
ourselves away. There's a satisfaction in knowing that you can deny
certain aspects of life—that somehow makes you full, more whole."

Fasting is an unselfish act. It can restore perspective in a world
gone greedy, affluent and excessive. Fasting gives us a taste of what

it means to willingly be hungry for a short period of time, knowing that there's plenty of food after the fast is over. Imagine what it is like to go hungry most of the time or all of the time, with no relief in sight. By denying ourselves, we foster empathy and compassion for those less fortunate than ourselves and ask ourselves, What can I do to alleviate the physical, spiritual and emotional hunger of the world? Islam has formalized the compassion induced by fasting. The last day of Ramadan Muslims pay a tax of one day's food for one person, so that the poor may also eat. One of the Five Pillars of Islam is alms giving, so in addition, Muslims must pay a 2½% tax each year to help take care of the poor.

A HEALTHY APPETITE FOR LIFE

Feasting and fasting in a religious context deepens our faith and can help us grow in our secular lives. What can they teach us in the secular realm? Perhaps these extremes can teach us about moderation, which is where it is prudent to spend most of our lives. Perhaps they can prompt us to ask ourselves: What if we did not overeat at every meal? What if, during the week, we stopped eating heavy desserts that are more appropriate for special occasions? Would we still need the forced fasting of a reducing diet? What if we ate a decent breakfast and lunch? Would we still gorge at dinner? Do we really want to continue eating fast food, or meat?

Gertrud Nelson, author of *To Dance with God* laments the degree to which fasting has been disregarded by the Christian Church. "Weight watching, diet fads, guilt-ridden calorie counting and a multitude of eating disorders rushed in" to fill the void, she writes. "It seems to me that the human condition struggles as much with a respect for what is flesh and blood as it does with relationship to the Spirit. What we do not undertake with consciousness overtakes us as a neurosis, an illness or a bad habit. While mortification is thought of today as sick or foolish, it is replaced by exactly the same disciplines we once disdained."

What if, the next time we undertake a religious fast, we used it as a springboard to change our relationship with food? What if we took time to enjoy food, if we ate more slowly and paid attention to the food rather than to the TV or a magazine? What if we made more effort to eat meals with our families?

Feasting and fasting can perk up our sensitivity to everything around us. What if we learned how to truly feast and use all our senses more fully? What if we fine-tuned our palate to appreciate the subtle tastes and textures of simple foods? And, as Rabbi Klenicki points out, "Technically, feasting refers to food, but symbolically it means enjoying all the richness of life." Tedeschi, too, says there are other kinds of feasting, for example, "on the word of God as revealed in the Scriptures. The whole thing is an embarrassment of riches." So, what if we feasted our eyes on beautiful trees, mountains, seasons and birds? What if we feasted our noses on the smell of flowers, essential oils, oranges and baking bread? What if we feasted our ears on beautiful music, a baby's gurgling, a cats purr? What if we let our fingertips softly and lingeringly caress pussy willows, silken clothes, a loved one's skin?

What if we expanded the definition of fasting and took a vacation from some of the things we really could do better without, such as bitterness, tardiness, thoughtlessness, rudeness? Popular author Rabbi Joseph Telushkin says his family regularly declares "a complaining fast" for three days or so. This, he says, stops the downward spiral of doom, gloom and whining and begins in the cycle of appreciating the good things that happen and cultivates an atmosphere of joy.

What if we purged our lives of foods, material things and emotions that we don't want and made room for those we do want? For one thing, the prophet Auntie Mame would have to eat her words: "Life is a banquet and most poor suckers are starving to death!"

6. *Solitude and Community*

In my room, the world is beyond my understanding.
But when I walk out I see that it
consists of three or four hills and a cloud.

—Wallace Stevens, "Of the Surface of Things"

That shudder of awe and delight with which the
individual soul always mingles with the universal soul.

—Ralph Waldo Emerson, *Essays: First Series*

Meet Betty Roi, chanteuse, dancer and yogi. If you were watching her as she practices the Iyengar style of hatha yoga, you would notice that her body movements are fluid, precise. Inhale. Exhale. Prana masana (prayer pose). Inhale. Exhale. Uttanasana (standing forward bend). Inhale. Exhale. Virabradrasana (warrior pose). Inhale. Exhale. Shvanasana (downward dog pose). Inhale. Exhale. Bhujangasana (cobra pose). She would also likely do Salamba Sarvangasana (shoulder stand), Chaturanga Dandasana (push up), Urdhva Mukha Svanasana (upward dog), Uttitha Trikonasana (triangle pose), Vrkasana (tree pose). These are all part of her daily yoga practice, and have been for nearly fifteen years.

Imagine you are watching her. Look closely: you will see the rise and fall of her belly with each breath, and a film of perspiration will appear on her supple, strong body as she flows from one pose to the next. The fluid beauty of the actions she performs and the poetry of the Sanskrit words for them belie the work she is ask-ing—demanding—of her body. But the effort of her body is noth-ing compared with what's going on in her mind and spirit. Look more closely. You will discern the look of rapt concentration on her face. With each pose, each breath, Roi is going deeper, deeper until she connects with what she calls "the vastness that is myself."

Despite outward appearances and hip articles in *People* mag-azine, yoga is not a get-fit-quick calisthenics workout or the lat-est way to stretch and relax. Rather, it is a serious full-fledged spiritual tradition, followed to varying degrees by Indians, Hindus and others who have taken on "the yoke." Roi says, "Yoga is a wonderful tool for happiness, for feeling more of a sense of freedom and joy in your life. When you can rest in the spaciousness of who you are, you have more equanimity, and you don't get rocked by the events of life."

Yoga is just one of the countless ways that we humans have been trying to get closer to God, and to even become one with the Absolute. Meditation, praying together, sharing rituals, singing, dancing, sacred sex, drugs, attending a house of wor-ship—we can use all of these things and more to forge a sense of community, hold back the horror of isolation and promote the altered states of consciousness that move us closer to whomever or whatever it is we want to be intimate with or become. That we should keep working at it in the same way humans have been practicing for thousands of years is a testament to its power and to a basic human hunger and need to connect with something larger than ourselves. Just as important is our need to discover and commune with our own essential selves and to feel a bond with our fellow humans. We are, as John of the Cross declared, "thirsty of God," thirsty of each other and thirsty of ourselves.

Some religions believe there essentially is no difference between the individual and God—we are God, God is us. God did not create us or the universe, God is everything. Others worship God as a separate entity and creator outside the self. No matter—in all religions the realization of this ultimate unity is a goal to be passionately desired and hopefully achieved for a few blissful moments, a lifetime or an eternity. Whether we yearn to meld into the universal soup or merely get closer to it and taste it, the question is: How do we get there and back again? How do we transcend our earthly selves, commune with God and our human community and not get permanently lost in the sublimity of it all? How does this change us and our lives? Can and should we still manage to remember to hold down a job and take out the trash? Is this a purely selfish act, or can some greater good come of it?

YEARNING TO BELONG, LONGING TO CONNECT

As Carolyn Shaffer and Kirsten Amondson eloquently reveal in their book, *Creating Community Anywhere*, the old forms of community—call it tribal identity or small town togetherness—have vanished. At a rate faster than the speed of light, marriages dissolve, families unravel, neighborhoods disintegrate. People drift off into their own worlds of loneliness and isolation, feeling left out and cast adrift, which can lead to detachment from the human race, and from the planet which we all share.

Today, almost a quarter of US households consist of people living alone. The American Dream of owning your own home, taking care of yourself, everyone minding his or her own business and rugged individualism haven't brought the happiness we thought it would. This form of individuality and freedom certainly has its price. Something is missing. Amidst all this splendor we yearn for something more—a sense of belonging of being connected to something larger, some sacred purpose.

The heartache of a lack of community these days is one reason why communal worship—where we can share our spiritual feelings, experiences, beliefs and rituals—is experiencing a surge in popularity. Religion can be the glue that binds people together.

As Frank Tedeschi, an Episcopalian who works for the Church Publishing Company states flatly, "Christianity is about relationships with yourself, with other people, with God." Physicists are saying the same thing: all matter, down to the smallest particle, exists in relation to itself. Nothing is fully knowable in isolation—it needs others to be complete and to be itself, whether the other is your fellow worshiper or the Great Spirit. In this sense, we are no different from the tiniest particle, the subtlest ripple in the energy of being.

As moderns we seem to think that we don't need transcendence. But such a primal need must come out somewhere. And it does: what are the ecstatic Superbowl vigils of Joe Six-Pack; the all-night "raves" of Gen X and Y; the be-ins and happenings of drug-infused hippies but crude attempts to duplicate spiritual excursions to the world beyond?

THE MYSTERY OF MYSTICISM

No matter what you call it—ecstasy, deification, bliss, beatific vision, *samadhi*, nirvana, *satori*—mystical union is sought after in all religious traditions, and all religions have a mystical aspect. Religions that were founded by or inspired by individuals owe their existence to the powerful personal mystical experiences of these individuals. Think of God speaking to Abraham; Jesus being both God and human and filled with the Holy Spirit; Siddhartha's enlightenment; Mohammed receiving the Qur'an Hindu seers instilled with the wisdom of the Vedas via mystical insight. But what are we talking about, exactly? Although humans have a long history of mapping the way to ecstasy we have always found it difficult to describe in words.

The Encyclopedia of Religion gives defining it the old college try: "A state of consciousness that surpasses ordinary experience through the union with a transcendent reality," and the "direct knowledge or immediate perception of the ultimate reality, or God," and "unification of man or man's soul with the highest reality." And: "Such union represents the supreme and most authentic elevation of the human spirit as it reaches a fusion with, or at least a living cognition of God or of the transcendent ground of being."

While these definitions may be accurate, and may suit all manner of experiences in all religious traditions, they hardly begin to convey the intensity, the joy, the fullness, the emptiness, the power, the eroticism, the exuberance, the exaltation, the wonder, the awe, or the sheer bliss and release one feels in this state of being. The plethora of literary, poetic and theological efforts comes closer. There, the common theme is sublimity, bliss and unsurpassable freedom in going beyond this limited, ordinary world and into a world with no boundaries of either time or space. A place where we can be perfect and infinite, from which we emerge psychologically rejuvenated, morally kinder and gentler, and creatively juicier. In other words, it's the greatest "high" and loftiest spiritual experience a human can experience. It is a "little death" that makes us feel alive. It is a glimpse of eternity.

The common denominator is the experience of at-oneness. Depending on the religious doctrine and view of God and the universe, this may involve uniting, or re-uniting; or it may involve the realization of a unity that already exists, but of which we are unaware. As might be expected, each religion has its own view of what's going on.

In many branches of Hinduism, one is seeking an Absolute Self; the individual soul or atman merges with Brahman, the whole, self-contained universe. This eventually leads to *moksha*, the freedom from the endless cycle of reincarnation. In Buddhism, the individual sees things as they really are and realizes that there is no individual soul, there is only the Ultimate Reality. There is no reuniting; there is only conscious awareness of the essence of things, a unity and oneness that is a state of utmost emptiness. The result of this enlightenment is *nirvana*—the end of the endless cycle of rebirth, and *the* spiritual goal in the Buddhist way of life.

Christianity does not seem to be terribly enthusiastic about mystical union, although a mystic thread does run through this tradition, beginning with Jesus and continuing up through all things Pentecostal. When it does appear, this intense intimacy with God is very much related to a feeling of universal love. The Christian mystic Bernard of Clair Vaux has described the highest degree of love as the condition of a drop of water disappearing into a vessel. And let us not forget that God so loved the world that He merged with human flesh and then gave us the Holy Spirit as a means of merging with Him. Islam, similarly, offers a love-mysticism, particularly among the Sufi sects, which emerged precisely in reaction to the sober, law-obsessed orthodoxy of this faith. In hymns and poetry and dance, the Sufis long for and express union with "the Beloved," in which one loses one's self, utterly. Judaism is an historic smorgasbord of mysticism, from the messianic Kabbalah to the joyful spirit of Hasidism. The common trait, if there is one, is an eschatological one—a mystical glimpse of the messianic kingdom to come.

In any tradition, there are generally two types of ecstatic union, one in which one "tastes sugar" and another in which one "becomes sugar." In the first, "communion," one merges with God, but remains a distinct individual; in the second "union," one becomes God. In this form of mystical experience, you are conscious that all is One; you feel totally immersed in the sacred natural universe, all differences are an illusion; you blend with the infinitesimal essences of energy of which reality is composed. All notions of duality—"I" and "It"—are dissolved. In other words, the distinction between experiencer and the experienced disappears. So, how and whom are you seeing? Meister Eckhart says, "The eye with which I see God is the same with which God sees me."

This type of experience goes far beyond our usual understanding of the words *ecstasy* or *bliss*, far beyond finally finding the perfect cappuccino, a bathing suit that fits, or the perfect masseuse or lover. As Georg Feuerstein writes in his book *Yoga*, "There is virtually nothing in our everyday life that could help us understand it . . . even the thrill of orgasm pales by comparison with the bliss of coming near, never mind merging with the Self." The experience is ineffable, because it lies beyond the realm of words. Perhaps to say that it is indescribable is the best way to describe it.

Reverend Cormier gives us a Christian's-eye-view of the "peak experience," which consists of "an acute consciousness of the presence of God, an intense awareness of this somehow absolute attention to me." The experience also includes "an intense sense that God has everything in his hands, and in the end everything is going to be all right." It involves a sense that "everything is one" and "adoration of God is an experience of God and His love" that is captivating in itself. The joy is just looking. It is a foretaste of the life to come," it is, he says, " the best thing I look forward to."

GETTING THERE

Now that we have some idea of where we are going, the question is: how do we get there? All religions have their paths, their tools, and their terminology. Yoga is perhaps the most holistic and comprehensive means of communing with the Infinite, as it consists of several approaches and a variety of techniques, many of which are also found in other traditions. It includes *hatha* yoga—the postures, poses or asanas with which the Western world has become so familiar. There are yoga classes all over, even in health clubs, plus videotapes, CDs, books and magazines devoted to the purely physical movement aspect of hatha yoga.

The purpose of yoga is to achieve a higher consciousness and a unity with the cosmos. Yogis practice yoga to find peace, quiet and stillness within . . . to go beyond the senses and calm the "monkey mind" that jumps around from thought to thought and sensation to sensation. Patanjali is credited with codifying yoga into a book called the *Yoga Sutras*. Five thousand years ago he described the four ways one could unite the soul with Brahman. Within these, the hatha yoga with which the West is most familiar is actually a relatively minor component.

The first path to mystic union is called *jnana yoga*, the path of knowledge. This involves studying sacred texts such as the Upanishads and Vedas. The next is called *bhakti yoga*, or the path of devotion. When you follow this path, you devote yourself to a deity, and are constantly remembering the divine with rituals, chanting, dancing and meditation. The third path is *karma yoga*, the path of action. This is the life dedicated to community service, doing good deeds without expecting anything in return. (Think of Mother Teresa.) The fourth path is that of *raja yoga*, the path of self-control. Hatha yoga is a part of raja yoga. Hatha means to "force" and it aptly describes the arduous physical purification and strengthening practices in which Betty Roi partakes. This form developed out of the realization that a healthy, strong, supple body can facilitate the journey to liberation better than a frail or diseased one.

But how does this all fit together to produce the much sought after cosmic high? We must turn to the word yoga itself. Yoga is derived from a Sanskrit word, *yug*, which means to "yoke or harness." This is usually interpreted as "joining" the consciousness of an individual self with the universal self. Yoga has also come to mean the union between an individual's body, mind and spirit. Yoga can also mean "discipline." In most instances, yoga means all these things: it is a discipline that unifies. According to the Bhagavad Gita, "the sage yoked in yoga soon attains the Absolute."

The hatha part has been likened to a moving meditation; a type of meditation that Roi says helped her to face the truth and deal with overwhelming emotions in her life. How can doing these postures have such a profound effect? "I think it is the quality of the presence of mind that it requires," she says. "Especially when you do Iyengar yoga, which is very precise about alignment, orientation and placement." Focusing so intently on the position of the head, hands, feet and hips, forces the mind to calm down and stop wandering. "It made me pay attention and be very present and absorbed in the moment." And when you do this, you eventually take a step back and witness yourself. You experience the sensation of "a Divine being that is having a human experience," says Roi.

The Rig-Veda couches this phenomenon in beautiful poetic mystical imagery: "The whole universe is stationed in your home within the ocean, within the heart, in life. May we gain your honey wave that is brought to the edge, the junction of the waters." We glimpse this junction through the hard work and discipline of yoga, Feuerstein explains. Yogic texts suggest that each yoga posture is sacred, and this sacredness transforms the body into a shrine for inner worship. Feuerstein says that when a posture is done successfully, you have the "sensation of extending beyond the skin, of being a vibrant energy field that imperceptibly merges with the environment."

Valuable as they are in and of themselves, hatha yoga postures are not an end in and of themselves; they are designed to condition the body to make prolonged sitting meditation possible. "You do yoga so your body will leave you alone," says Roi. "Most people in the West cannot sit still even for five minutes on a chair, let alone on the floor or a pillow. The body is screaming, the back hurts, the knees hurt." And yet the sitting lotus position that folds your legs like a pretzel is ideal because it allows you to keep the spine correctly aligned. Kundalini is the "serpent power" that lies coiled in the lowest chakra (psychospiritual center) of the body. During lotus, "your pelvis is heavy, you have the feeling of being effortlessly and completely erect so the chakras are in alignment and the Kundalini energy can rise up unimpeded," Roi explains, to the highest chakra at the crown of the head.

"The most important aspect of asana practice is the proper regulation of the breath," Feuerstein tells us." Breath control (*pranayama*) and other hatha yoga practices are meant to purify and stabilize the energy of the body, and to prepare the body for awakening the kundalini. The ancients define prana as breath energy plus a universal energy. Most people's breathing pattern is irregular, shallow, haphazard, making for erratic shallow thinking. Yoga-pranayama corrects this. Yogic breath control is not simply a manipulation of the intake of oxygen into our lungs but a technique for regulating the flow of your inner force and your mental processes. Feuerstein adds, "Through breath control the yogi energizes and harmonizes the body and thus creates a solid foundation for mental concentration and the induction of higher states of consciousness, as well as the complete transcendence of the body mind in the moment of enlightenment."

The rhythm of the pranayama breath also affects your state of consciousness; the slower the rhythm, the deeper you can penetrate certain states of consciousness without losing your clarity of thought and the greater your ability to concentrate. In Roi's experience, "the breath is a powerful tool for bringing you from the external world to the internal world."

The discipline of yoga includes meditation, a practice that also exists in some form in all other spiritual paths as well. Meditation involves concentration, which allows you to narrow your conscious focus to one thing: an object such as an image of a deity, a flame, a word, idea, and so on. Sometimes a distinction is made between meditation and contemplation; a twelfth-century Christian theologian distinguished the two this way: "Meditation investigates, contemplation wonders." That's something to contemplate.

In Buddhism, you attain the unity of nirvana through moral discipline and mental concentration involving the confrontation of paradoxes and meditation. The Zen School of Buddhism is famous for its *koans*: paradoxical statements that perplex the mind of reason, and which can only be "solved" if one can find a "higher" sense. This process clears the mind of ordinary thoughts, allowing unconscious thoughts to emerge.

Reverend Kobutsu Malone says, "In Zen, the real essence is the practice of zazen, the seated contemplative meditative practice." Each year he attends a 90-day and a 100-day training period. Each training period consists of a number of seven-day intense retreats during which he sits hour after hour, all day long. "The purpose is to engage in extensive zazen practice with no distractions," he says. "It's a very fierce, extremely difficult practice, physically and psychologically demanding. It makes EST look like the Boy Scouts." Why does he do it? "Because it works. It enables one to see and penetrate into one's own nature, to see how things are."

Judaism, Christianity and Islam rely primarily on prayer as a form of meditation and contemplation. In addition, Judaism has several related traditions such as the intense study of and meditation on the Hebrew Scriptures. In the Hasidic tradition, one contemplates the spirit of the living God; God can't be contemplated directly until the end of the world, Judgment Day. In any event, there is no mystical union, rather a sense of being joined to God as a totally separate entity. Abulafia, an exponent of the Kabbalistic School, developed a unique system of meditation based on the letters of the Hebrew alphabet as the object of concentration. B'nai Jeshurun's Rabbi Bronstein says that the mystical tradition developed many techniques of personal connection with God. "This is an historic moment in Jewish tradition because we are recovering the whole meditative-contemplative tradition. This tradition goes back to the twelfth and thirteenth centuries, but was forgotten in the Enlightenment, and many of the teachers were killed in the Holocaust."

When one thinks of Christian meditation, one generally thinks of monks, who developed a high degree of sophistication in their practices. Christian meditation is rich in images of mystical ascent to divine knowledge, an absorption in the One, achieved by a spiritual trek up the ladder of perfection. Ignatius, founder of the Jesuits, developed a meditative method that involves choosing a specific image and then mentally immersing yourself in a sensual orgy of that image—seeing, hearing, tasting, smelling and touching it—until it becomes alive in your consciousness. This is very similar to the visualization technique used in Hinduism, which culminates in the meditator identifying with the image of the imagined deity so strongly and clearly that he or she *becomes* the deity.

Of course there are other tools for ecstasy, including sound and movement, and two highly controversial ones: sex and drugs. Most often it is the absence of sex that is the tool for enlightenment: celibacy is part of many traditions from the nunnery to the ashram. In these cases abstinence is a component of the ascetic life, a life free of distractions, a life in which the energy and attention that might be otherwise squandered on earthly activities is channeled to spiritual ones. But there is another tradition, one in which sex is a significant part of the quest for ecstatic union. For example, in left-hand tantrism, sexual intercourse is a technique coupled with meditation used to alter consciousness, with the act of intercourse representing the integration of matter and spirit.

In spite of its uptight image, sex is no stranger to Christian mystical ecstasy. Teresa of Avila is renowned for her vivid descriptions of her mystical inner ecstatic experiences. This Carmelite nun's meditations take the form of sexual images and incorporate the symbolism of bride and bridegroom for that of union. This type of sublime sublimation of sexual fever into religious fervor is the stuff that memoirs and lurid movies are made of. But what about "real" honest-to-goodness carnal sex with bodies in fleshy sexual union? There are those who would elevate such coupling to the divine, with some theologians seeing in sexual encounter a foretaste of the eternal life of heaven. Ronald Rolheiser, in his book *The Holy Longing*, describes sexuality as "a beautiful, good, extremely powerful, sacred energy, given us by God and experienced in every cell of our being as an irrepressible urge to overcome our incompleteness, to move toward unity and consummation with that which is beyond us. . . . Christianity must have the courage to let go of some of its fears and timidities and learn to celebrate the goodness of sexual passion," Rolheiser proclaims.

Islam, with its paradoxical traditions of love mysticism and extreme protectiveness of women, is no stranger to spiritual sexual love, either. Ibn al-Arabi, a Muslim mystic, believed that sexual intimacy can provide access to the perfect love of God, and that in woman, man most perfectly contemplates God. He writes, "The greatest union is that between man and woman, corresponding as it does to the turning of God toward the one He has created in His own image . . . so that He might behold Himself in him."

But few if any link the sacred with erotic longing and joining more poetically than Jalaludin Rumi, the thirteenth-century Sufi mystic and founder of the whirling dervishes. For example, one of his poems contains these lines: "The engagement, the coming together, is as with the lion . . . and their two spirits go out from them as one . . . Whenever two are linked this way, there comes another from the unseen world . . . The intense qualities born of such joining appear in the spirit world."

So sometimes the Divine can be found between the sheets; can it be found in a bottle, or a cup or a pipe? "Oh, like, wow! Yeah, man," say a long line of experimenters of mind altering chemicals from the soma-sipping Hindus of Vedic times to the more recent seekers of the truth via mushrooms, cactus, LSD and most recently the aptly named lab-produced Ecstasy. However, mystical union is not simply an altered state of consciousness; it is not to be equated with hallucinatory "trips" or trances induced by drugs. The language used to describe such experiences may sound similar to religious ecstasy, but this is the fault of the language, which is limited.

Also, not all such "trips" are ecstatic.

And finally, chemically induced ecstasy, unlike a mystical experience, rarely transforms the experiencer into a wiser, holier, clearer thinking, compassionate person. Rather, he is usually cranky and fuzzy headed the next day—and that's if he's lucky. Drugs may, in some people, under the right conditions, help trigger or facilitate a mystical trance; but as is the case with the asanas of yoga, the ladder up should not be confused with the heavenly destination itself.

And what is one to make of the rite of Holy Communion, the centerpiece of Christian worship? "This is my body, this is my blood," said Christ as he offered the bread and the wine to his Apostles during the Last Supper. The bread, the wine, once consecrated and ingested, are believed to transfuse spiritual energy from God to the human soul, perhaps by transubstantiation. This is a technique and a type of unity that is unique among the major religions. In *Christianity for Beginners*, Ralph Milton writes, that this sacrament of the Church is a symbolic action, the Christian community sharing a symbolic meal. Each time we gather for the Eucharist "we not only remember Jesus, but in a very special and particular way we become a part of him—or he becomes a part of us." To Milton the Eucharist means different things at different times, "Sometimes, it seems to be a nice, warm celebration of the community we share in the Church. Sometimes I simply know that I am deeply in touch with the holy, the mysterious, the eternal."

Certainly something biochemical transpires in the state of

ecstasy. Scientists are fascinated by altered states of consciousness and religious ecstasy. They are using biofeedback devices
and monitoring endorphin levels to study this phenomenon. It
seems the right hemisphere of the brain is where these states are
produced, and this is the "nonverbal" half of the brain, which
may also help account for the ineffability of these experiences.

ALONE, TOGETHER

Most of the means to ecstatic union with God involve solitary activities such as praying, meditation, contemplation, solo pilgrimages
and wandering in the wilderness. Most religions have ascetics and
monks who live lives of seclusion, quiet simplicity and solitude. As
Trappist monk and author Thomas Merton writes, " I have really
only one desire and that is the desire for solitude—to disappear into
God, to be submerged in His peace, to be lost in the secret of His
face." Centuries before Merton took pen to paper, the original Sufis
were hermits— "lone rangers"—says Latif Bolat, a Sufi musician.
"Solitude was a better way to get into the message of the word." As
an example of the lengths to which some ascetics will go, he presents us with Rabia, an early Sufi monk from Iraq: "Legend has it she
wouldn't even open her windows because she said the beautiful sunshine is a distraction from her devotion to Allah."

Hinduism, of course, has a tradition of lone meditators, but
worship service in a Hindu temple offers a disciplinary challenge,
says Dr. Anand Mohan, associate professor at Queens College.
The service itself is a spectacle—part theater, part esthetic enjoyment. There is a cacophony of sound—chanting, praying,
singing, bells clanging. There is the chaos of kids running
around, people constantly on the move, going from one deity to
another, cracking open coconuts as offerings, washing fruit,
deities being washed, incense burning. Yet "even amidst all that
chaos, you, the individual worshiper are in intimate contact with

your deity and nothing should disturb you, or annoy you. You should be in control of yourself," says Dr. Mohan. "Because in everyday life, you do not have perfect, undisturbed peace. It will not happen. So, like in the temple, in the middle of this chaotic, unintelligible world, you should be able to extricate yourself from all of that" and be able to focus inward in solitude, he says.

Few of us would run off to a monastery to experience the long-term quiet solitude of a Merton or deprive ourselves of sunlight like Rabia. But we all need *some* time alone, *some* time away, whether we realize it or not. Solitude, even when we don't spend it contemplating spiritual matters is delightful—emotionally, physically and spiritually. Solitude is a respite from the overstimulation of a too-busy, too-populated life. Time alone rejuvenates and restores the juices. It gives us a chance to solve problems, make peace with ourself, to reflect on things great and small. It allows us to think vigorously and deeply without interruption. In the process, we find an inner ease and repose that brings us closer to ourself and improves our relationships with other mortals as well as the Infinite.

If we don't give ourselves time alone, we experience the classic effects of stress: anxiety, sleep disturbances, irritability, burnout, depression, lowered productivity and psychosomatic symptoms. On the other hand, studies show that the types of restriction of environmental stimulation such as that experienced on lone voyages and isolated wilderness jobs have measurable physiological effects similar to deep relaxation. These include lowered heart and respiration rate, lowered blood pressure and muscle tension and reduced levels of stress hormones. These effects also resemble those found during transcendental meditation, the form of meditation that has been most extensively studied. Whether it takes the form of prayer, meditation or a quiet walk in nature, most people find it helps to regularly schedule their daily dose of solitude, just like any important appointment. This way, they set up a pattern that becomes ingrained and establish a rhythm of expectation and fulfillment that the mind and body loves and needs.

Solitude is sweet, but union with our fellow humans has its own delights, and is a great reinforcer of religious beliefs. The Abrahamic religions all have a strong sense of religious community. In Judaism there is the traditional notion of the Hebrew nation; in Christianity the Church is the body of Christ; in Islam, the community of the faithful and the Islamic brotherhood.

Wayne Dosick writes:

Judaism is much more than a religion . . . it is also a people-hood—a group of people linked, much like any other nation, by history, language, literature, land, culture, and common destiny. Judaism is a group of people sharing an identity and sense of belonging, rootedness and authenticity, mutual responsibility and mutual benefit . . . It is this interdependence of religion and peoplehood that has given Judaism its unique greatness and has sustained it throughout the generations.

To which Rabbi Bronstein adds, "You will find very interesting characters in Judaism. There are people who say, 'I hate the rabbis, I hate the synagogue, I never go to Yom Kippur—in fact, I eat barbecue on Yom Kippur.' And yet they say they feel very Jewish. Judaism is not a religion of the individual, of personal faith. It's about a common destiny of a people . . . the traditions, the language, the culture, the music."

"In Judaism, community is paramount," says Rabbi Leon Klenicki, director of Interfaith Affairs at the Anti-Defamation League in New York. "Our traditions do solidify the sense of a united community. When we pray, many of the prayers are in the plural—*we* have transgressed, save *us*, bless *us*. And it is more meaningful to pray together in a synagogue because you are part of a community" he says. He∙ is referring to the centuries-old tradition of the *minyan*—or prayer group that requires ten men—in Jewish orthodoxy. This tradition is so powerful because it is a form of community prayer.

In a paper published in 1997 by S. Scheidlinger, the author focused on an aspect of this weekly prayer group, particularly the "rarely recognized, nonliturgical dimension." He observed that the minyan functions as a psychological support system that gratifies social hunger, counters loneliness and isolation and helps members maintain an intergenerational sense of personal identity and self-esteem. He concludes, "The earlier emphasis in Western cultures on the virtual worship of individuality, autonomy and independence has given way recently to a renewed appreciation of cooperation, communalism, and altruism." From his lips to God's ears.

But what about faiths that exist in a world that is growing more multicultural every day? Can a common faith be the thread that ties diverse people together, that unites them by sharing rituals, prayers and creating a new history together? Sharon Blackburn, minister of the Plymouth Church of the Pilgrims, says,

It's very easy to practice the Christian faith in isolation. It's not so easy in the real world, in relationships, because we are tested. It's easy to love the stranger across the street, but in a church community, you are forced to walk together. It's where the rubber hits the road, because we all have our prickles. But the purpose of Christianity is to teach us how to be together. The Church has the most potential of anything to bring peace to the world.

Frank Tedeschi does not see ethnic diversity as an insurmountable challenge. After all, he says, "community is a major, ancient Christian concept; the earliest Christian Church was a community and today there are still Christian communes." He continues: "No two of us are alike, really—we are separate as individuals but one in Christ; we are all created in God's image. The reality of Christian life is that there is unity in diversity—you are totally special in God's eyes. Even your hairs are numbered—this shows us how carefully each one of us is created and how intimately each one of us is loved."

Ronheiser sees church community as a "practice for heaven." He writes, "Heaven, the Scriptures assure us, will be enjoyed within the communal embrace of billions of persons of every temperament, race, background, and ideology imaginable. A universal heart will be required to live there. Thus, in this life, it is good to get some practice at this, good to be constantly in situations that painfully stretch the heart. Few things—and we certainly all admit this—stretch the heart as painfully as does church community."

Reverend Robert Cormier, associate pastor of a large New Jersey parish, has noticed that "life is better when we get together. God constructed us in a way that our life would always be one in which we share." He adds that we feel more sure of things when we are in church together. "You're thinking: all those people are of the same faith, making the same judgments. Numbers increase our faith." Cormier believes when we ask people to pray for us, we are really asking for companionship. "We are asking others to care with me, hope with me! In this everyone gains—anything is lighter if many people carry it. So we get a lighter load. [And] others get to love," he writes in *A Faith That Makes Sense*.

Islamic rituals also instill a sense of fellowship among adherents—especially the five-times-a-day prayer. No matter where a Muslim may be, he or she is reassured that millions of other Muslims are facing Mecca, participating all over the world in the same actions and saying the same words, one time zone after another, like a huge wave continually traversing the globe, in a communal recognition of Allah and His power. Communal praying in a mosque, which is required once a week, allows Muslims to come together in dignity and social equality not available in the outside world.

The once-in-a-lifetime pilgrimage to Mecca is an even greater equalizing and bonding opportunity. As Thomas Lippman writes in *Understanding Islam*, "Rich or poor, herdsman and tycoon, scholar and illiterate, man and woman, Arab, Persian, and Turk, African and Asian journey to the sacred shrine. Some camp in tents, others stay in new hotel suites at exorbitant prices, but all are equal before Allah as they kneel in prayer, indistinguishable in the white raiment of pilgrimage." And once it's over, "Each participant has taken part in a human migration and collective spiritual exercise that knows no parallel in Western faith. The Hajj represents a spiritual triumph that brings together more than a million souls, united in their exhalation and their devotion to Allah and his prophet."

The Eastern traditions have a different flavor of community. In Buddhism, sometimes when we come together to "meditate communally, we call it being alone together on the cushion," says Kobutsu Malone, a Zen Buddhist priest. "Meditating together supports our discipline, it supports our heart nature. We are sitting communally; we are responsible to our neighbors and our friends sitting next to us—what we call our brotherhood, or *sangha*. We are responsible for remaining quiet, for maintaining the sitting posture without squirming, for toughing it out because to do otherwise would disturb and distract others."

"What we have in Hinduism are cults and sects—you smear ashes on your forehead one way if you worship one deity, and another way for another deity," says Mohan. "What is deeply rooted in the Hindu worldview is that individuals are part of a larger organism and the whole is sustained by its part through sacrifice. So for the sake of the family you must sacrifice yourself; for the sake of the group you sacrifice the family; for the sake of the village, you must sacrifice the group," and so on through the religion, county and whole world. Buddhism shares much with this Hindu worldview of the individual and the larger whole.

THE FRUITS

And once you have tasted the delights of transcendence, communed with God, or perhaps even reached enlightenment—then what? It would be a sorry state of affairs if all this amounted to was a bunch of beaming transformed beings sitting around contemplating their navels, oblivious to the rest of the world going to hell in a handbasket. Some people, such as Pir Vilayat Inayat Khan, author of *Awakening: A Sufi Experience*, believe that,

> As individuals alter their consciousness, so too do they effect a transformation in the surrounding environment. This represents a breathtaking breakthrough that radically distinguishes the spirituality of the future from that of the past. The Universe is evolving toward an even greater global destiny—and we are the means of this global transformation!

Perhaps this grand vision will come about through spiritual or mental effort alone. Physicists think it's possible. Perhaps change will happen another way. Enlightenment is a spiritual path and a lifelong discipline that includes moral wisdom and action. Fortunately in most disciplines, enlightenment is more than a state of *being*; it is a state of *doing*. Your behavior—talking, working, eating, relationships with other people, as well as meditation—constantly manifests your inner state. A moral, compassionate way of life facilitates enlightenment, as well as grows out of it.

For example, since Christian mysticism and union with God is based on love, the enlightened Christian increases in his love for his neighbor. When one receives grace of God, one becomes more like God, and presumably more loving, compassionate and caring. In the Jewish tradition, we are put on earth to "repair the world" and do good works to reverse injustices.

A Buddhist may "know" that "all is nothing," and seeking

nirvana may be equated with escapism, but in most Buddhist schools, enlightenment is more than an insight or even a sense of harmony. It is also a mode of behavior to be continuously enacted and tested in every day life. Enlightenment both requires and deepens compassion because of the profound connectedness of all things. The Buddhist way of life, also called the Eightfold Path, is an all-encompassing code of attitude, lifestyle, and spiritual practice. "Right view" is the realization of interconnectedness of everything. "Right intentions" is a committed engagement to the path. "Right speech" is truthful, gentle, constructive and purposeful. "Right action" includes compassion and goodwill. "Right livelihood" means bad behavior is not okay because it's "just business." "Right effort" means making the effort to follow these principles. "Right mindfulness" means cultivating awareness. And "Right contemplation" is meditating to calm the mind and harmonize urges.

In Yoga, morality is inseparable from metaphysics—it is a strict discipline that also has a strong moral foundation because yoga recognizes the universal self in all beings. Feuerstein says, "Yoga practitioners do not choose a moral way of life merely for their own convenience. Rather they view their moral life as an obligation to the larger good by respecting a cosmic pattern of harmony in which all beings can flourish and find their true identity." In other words, it is impossible to be enlightened and psychologically abuse your spouse or children, to steal, to be arrogant and prideful, to be greedy or to lie. The same moral code is found in all the great religions of the world, but yoga is unique in that it must caution its practitioners not to lose sight of this basic truth and take pride in doing a head stand; to flaunt tight muscle tone; to get caught up in esoteric hygiene practices or to toy with tantric sex and other Kundalini delights.

On the matter of individuals incorporating the rhythm of solitude and community, heavenly bliss and earthly reality, into their lives, Dr. Mohan has the last word. He tells the story of a wise woman who was asked: What happens after you attain Nirvana? She said, "You have to do the laundry." In other words, you reengage in your material life. "The world hasn't changed, but your attitude toward it—*that* is transformed, and *you* are transformed so it never looks the same again," says Mohan. Although you have gone beyond the values of good and evil, the world has not, and we must abide by a code of conduct. You cannot resort to nihilism or cynicism and say nothing matters—it does matter. That instant of illumination has permanently changed you, but you are still in the world." One needs to do one's laundry, yes. But perhaps the true test of enlightenment is whether one also offers to do the dirty laundry of one's needy neighbor.

7. Celebration and Mourning

God hath not granted to woeful mortals even laughter without tears.

—Callimachus, *Fragments*

*Every act of creation
is first of all
an act of destruction.*

—Pablo Picasso

The year was 1969. The United States was at war in Vietnam. Irvin Ungar remembers with crystal clarity that chilling day in December, when the US government held the first draft lottery. The news for him, a young college student with his whole life ahead of him, was bad, extremely bad. "My number was very low and that meant that I was scheduled to go to Vietnam," he recalls. "I called my mother that night. She was crying, devastated, 'What are you going to do? What are we going to do?' For consolation and advice, she talked to our rabbi. He suggested that I go to divinity school because that merited a 4-D exemption." So Ungar, who was majoring in math and economics at the time, which some might say is as far from a divine calling as you can get, went off to rabbinical school.

"The bad luck of the draft lottery changed my life," he says. "As it turns out, I became a very good divinity student. I really loved it. And I became a rabbi, and I loved that." Instead of donning a uniform and toting weapons of war, Ungar donned the tallis and embraced the Torah. "The moral of this story," Ungar says, "is that God works in mysterious ways and no matter how you plan, your life can suddenly change directions." And change again: after thirteen years as a "pulpit rabbi" he switched careers and has found joy and satisfaction elsewhere. He is now the owner of Historicana Rare Books and Manuscripts, and works with the artist Arthur Szyk, serving as curator of his work at numerous museum exhibitions and president of the Arthur Szyk Society. He's finally a businessman, but a businessman with a spiritual mission. God works in mysterious ways, indeed.

Ungar, like so many people, has experienced the sometimes dizzying pendulum swings of life: from happy, carefree college student to terrified potential Vietnam cannon fodder, from valued spiritual counselor to museum curator. Most of us live lives that are similar checkerboards of change, of gain and loss—things that make us joyful and eager to celebrate, and things that cause us to suffer and mourn. Loved ones, jobs, income, friends, homes, pets, material goods, security, comfort—these blessings come and go and, we hope, come again as part of the crazy jazz-rhythm of life.

Most religions have myths about a time when there was only goodness and happiness in the world, a paradise in which life was perfect. So we humans have a powerful image of life as we think it should be—a life in which there is no evil, in which we do not mourn or suffer, a life like that lived by people in some long-lost past, or like some longed-for, hoped-for life of the future. But in real life, we do suffer, we do mourn, evil does exist. This tendency for the sunnyness of joy to be shadowed by suffering is a rhythm that—more than all others—prompts us to ask the kinds of soul-searching questions that plumb the very depths of our religious beliefs. Extreme suffering can shake our faith, even destroy it; conversely, adversity can strengthen our belief beyond all understanding. Bad times make us examine more profoundly our inner selves and the foundations of what we believe in. The fact that humans have much to celebrate but also suffer so mightily raises a difficult problem that has prompted billions of thoughts, words and gallons of ink to flow from the pens of the greatest thinkers of all time as well as from many ordinary people who have suffered a great loss. Few people need an explanation for goodness, or have trouble coping with good fortune. Yes, it's good to be alive and we have much to be happy about. But why, oh why does life have to hurt so much, too? Long before psychotherapy was invented, religious practices and beliefs have tried to offer guidance and a safe haven to generations of confused souls.

THE PROBLEM OF EVIL

The "problem of evil" is a huge one for anyone who believes in a wise, good, loving Creator. It leads you to a stream of questions that could keep you occupied for a lifetime. Here are a few: If there is a God, and this God controls everything, and if there is meaning and purpose to existence, then why did He create evil and suffering? Why didn't He create life only full of joy? Does it mean God is limited in power? Does it mean He doesn't love us or care about us? Does suffering have a purpose in His Divine Plan, a purpose we cannot see or comprehend? Why do bad things happen to good people? Why are bad people rewarded rather than punished? Why is there such injustice in the world? If God did not create evil, who did? The Devil? Does that mean the Devil is as powerful as God—is the Devil a god, too?

Religions respond to the problem of evil in several ways. They try to explain the existence of suffering and evil in the context of their philosophy—as part of the nature, meaning and purpose of life. And they offer moral guidelines and specific practices to prevent and alleviate suffering in our personal lives and in the world in general. These guidelines and practices usually include compassion for those who are less fortunate than we are, which leads to actions to alleviate their suffering. Religious moral principles attempt to curb humans' baser instincts that might hurt others, and thus prevent much of our suffering in the first place. For example, Hindus follow the principle of dharma and Buddhists follow the Eightfold Path; Islam emphasizes charity towards others as one of its Five Pillars of the faith; Judaism and Christianity have the Ten Commandments. These two approaches, one philosophical, the other practical, are often interwoven and interdependent. Together they offer a lifeboat—albeit a rather leaky one—that aims to help us to stay afloat in the raging sea of life.

Most diseases and accidents, fires, earthquakes, tornadoes, old age and death are due to natural causes—these are examples of "natural" evil because they are events outside human control. People used to believe that natural events were directly related to the way people behaved. So, for example, God said to the Jews if they obeyed the Ten Commandments, "I would give you the rain of the land in your season." Similarly, drought, earthquakes and floods were thought to be God's punishment for wrongdoing. Today most people prefer the explanation that these so-called "acts of God" are really just the laws of nature in action.

Moral evil on the other hand signifies suffering human beings inflict on each other: violence, rape, robbery, cruel words, lies, war, betrayal, disrespect. Many argue that moral evil exists because without the possibility of evil there would be no free will—if there were only goodness to choose from, there would be no real choice. On the other hand, perhaps God did not create a world of suffering. Frank Tedeschi, the managing editor of the Church

Publishing Company, says, "Human beings missed the point in the glory of creation and misused that power. That is what original sin is all about. We suffer because of Adam and Eve."

OUT OF EVIL, GOODNESS?

One of the strongest religious justifications for evil—even natural evil—is that suffering is by God's design; it is for an ultimate good cause and some of it is even necessary. What good could possibly come out of evil? Or suffering? Well, for one thing, as we meet with suffering, we learn. It is an educational tool that makes us stretch and grow. It is a challenge that leads to self-examination, self-discovery, greater insight, and compassion and concern for others rather than concern for our own welfare and interests. Peter Stoltzfus, minister of music at Plymouth Church of the Pilgrims, says, "If everything were perfect, we wouldn't grow and develop into all that we can become. There has to be grist for the mill." Reverend Sharon Blackburn of the same church remembers that when she was fired from a job, it helped her "come to a different understanding of myself. God used the experience of my getting fired to show a side of me that I'm not proud about now. I'm human, and it was a growth." To paraphrase Neitzche, that which does not make you shrivel up into a little ball of pain and woe will make you a stronger, better person.

Some people believe that God bestows the experience of pain and suffering on people who are able to bear this burden—the strong take on the burdens of others. For example, the Jewish people believe in *tikkun olam*—"the repair of the world"—as their purpose in life. If the world were perfect, there would be nothing to repair, no sacred work to be done. God has chosen the Israelites to rise to the occasion and do good deeds to make the world a better place and alleviate suffering on a global scale as well as an intimate one. As is written in Isaiah 42:6–7: "I have given you as a

light to the nations, to open the eyes that are blind, to bring out
the prisoners from the dungeon, from the prison those who sit in
the darkness." This too, in a way, is ultimately good.

Perhaps evil or sin exists to make goodness all the sweeter.
One of Jesus' parables is the story of the prodigal son, who fool-
ishly squanders his inheritance and is forced to make a living
feeding pigs. Repentant, he finally returns home to his father,
who misses him greatly. The father welcomes him with open
arms, annoying the older son who never strayed. To the older
son the father says, "you were always with me, but I have to celebrate and rejoice in the return of your brother, because he was
dead and has come back to life; he was lost and now is found."
Perhaps, when we sin and repent, God is pleased with us as the
father was with the prodigal son.

In one of his poems, the Sufi poet Rumi tells the story of
Muhammad who rose one morning to see an eagle flying away
with his boot. As he was mourning the loss of his boot,
Muhammad saw that the boot turned upside down and a snake
fell out, thus saving the prophet from a poisonous snakebite. In
the poem Rumi says that Sufism is "the feeling of joy when sudden disappointment comes," and closes the poem by admonish-
ing us not to grieve for what doesn't come and that "some things
that don't happen keep disasters from happening."

Cliché though they may be, the expressions "every cloud has a
silver lining" and "every time it rains, it rains pennies from heav-
en," are right on target in their choice of weather as metaphor for
uncontrollable misfortune. Along these same lines, we have the
religious notion that "everything happens for the best," which is
sometimes translated into "God works in mysterious ways" by the
traditionalists and "there are no accidents" by New Agers. Ungar's
sudden calling as a rabbi falls under this category.

So do all the people who come to find meaning in personal
adversity by volunteering for or founding activist organizations

that aim to stamp out whatever particular scourge afflicted them or their loved one. This reasoning may be the only way possible of justifying the anguish of, for example, losing a child—by instilling meaning into the experience so it didn't happen "for nothing." But, as Harold Kushner concludes in his book *When Bad Things Happen to Good People*, "There is a crucial difference between denying the tragedy, insisting that everything is for the best, and seeing the tragedy in the context of a whole life, keeping one's eye and mind on what has enriched you and not only on what you have lost."

DON'T ASK

Theoretically, we could stamp out moral evil if everyone followed the moral principles preached by religion. However, natural evil would still plague us. And it still wouldn't answer the question as to why the world was made in such a way that moral evil could exist— why create humans that would intentionally cause people to suffer? And what about the randomness of evil? Why is one baby born with a horrible defect and another with a silver spoon in his mouth? Why does one person get struck with cancer, or hit by a truck—and not another? Can squeezing the juice of goodness and joy out of the turnip of evil and suffering truly justify all the babies who are born with terrible defects and live lives that are nasty, brutal and very short? Or the pain suffered by innocent people in volcanoes, hurricanes, fires and wars? Does God single out certain people for joy or sorrow, or did He simply create the laws of nature, which are irrevocable and afflict everyone equally and randomly?

These are just too many questions. Clearly, sometimes we can't find meaning or goodness in evil. For example, the Holocaust forced all Jews, particularly the survivors of the extermination camps, to ask, "Where was God?" How could humans be so evil, so cruel to other human beings? Some Jews responded by abandoning God and the covenant, feeling that God had abandoned them. Some became "more Jewish," and redoubled their study of the Talmud, or decided to support right-wing orthodoxy. Others went on to help create the State of Israel. But, writes Dosick in *Living Judaism*, when it comes right down to the reason for evil, "Judaism says plainly: We do not know, because we are not God. We do not know God's ways, for they are beyond our understanding."

This is remarkably close to Islam, which says simply, "What's all the fuss about? God has absolute control over everything, therefore both good and evil, joy and suffering, are simply his will." Even though Allah writes your destiny on your forehead, the Islamic view includes that of suffering as a punishment and happiness as a reward for behavior. Lack of belief is the root of misbehavior and hence, of evil. Suffering is also a test of faith, and the way you deal with your tribulations reveals to God your innermost soul. Because of their strong moral code, Muslims are commanded to endure their own suffering, no questions asked, and work to alleviate the suffering of others.

NOT SO INSTANT KARMA

Three thousand years or so ago, Vedic seers in the subcontinent of India divined the concept of *karma*. Today, karma is on everyone's lips, whether or not they truly understand its subtleties. Karma explains the origin and cause of suffering and of both types of evil; it explains both immediate and delayed gratification and suffering and it explains the seeming randomness of it all. "The notion of karma enables us to cope with so many things for which other people might say 'Why did God create this wretched world? Was he stupid? Couldn't he do better than this?' So we have the concept of karma, to explain every blessed thing," says Dr. Anand Mohan, a professor of philosophy and religious studies at Queens College in New York. Mohan explains that there are three kinds of karma.

The one everyone is familiar with is the karma of things you have done. Put in the simplest terms possible, karma is the result of action. Good deeds bring good karma and good fortune, happiness, etc. Bad deeds bring on bad karma and bad fortune, suffering, etc. So why do bad things happen to good people, and vice-versa? Karma has an explanation: because of reincarnation, your deeds from past lives carry over into this lifetime. Thus, moral evil does eventually get punished, but it may take several lifetimes for this to come to fruition. Moral good is also eventually rewarded. This philosophy also takes care of suffering from natural evil, because those who are victims of hurricanes and so on are reaping karma created in previous lives.

Mohan gives the infamous O.J. Simpson, who was acquitted of the brutal slayings of his wife and her lover, as an example. "He is free, but suppose he is guilty? He got away, partly because of the aspects of his good karma that he should not suffer in this life. Does that mean he is going to go scot-free forever? No! The consequences of that will have to be paid at some point, and in the next life." In this lifetime, there is nothing you can do about this type of karma, explains Mohan.

However, you can change the other two types of karma. You have total freedom in forming the karma that gives you your personality, and in the third karma, which is the way you prepare for your next life. "Karma is not fate, it is action, and you can take the necessary action to surmount aspects of karma," says Mohan. "Karma says we are all made of tendencies, propensities, proclivities. Just as we desired and made these in an earlier life, we can undesire them in this life, and remake ourselves. You can change your attitude. When your attitude changes, happiness and suffering are still there, but you look at them differently."

How does this karma business help you cope with a great

loss, such as the loss of a child? Dr. Mohan explains:

> If you wallow in your self pity and depression—this creates your personality, your tendencies that you will be born with in your next life. You won't even know why you are feeling a certain way—why am I suffering so, why am I like this? But you can change this now. You can think: That child of mine who I loved so dearly has her own journey to go on, her own karma. I can do nothing about her karma. But I can do something about mine. How do I take this loss? Do I take it creatively? Do I take it like Christ on the cross? Do I look at the suffering of others and realize how lucky I am because there are millions of people suffering far more intensely than I am? Can I share their suffering? There should be no denial or rejection of these feelings, there should be acceptance and overcoming.

This immense achievement comes about through the tools of enlightenment.

Buddhism and Hinduism share the notion of karma and of the impermanence of life, and of everything. You should not form attachments because "whatever you have, it is not yours. Whatever you feel—you enjoy happiness, but you know it is ephemeral—it is not going to last forever. And when you suffer and mourn—that's not going to last either. And if it does last, as in cases of prolonged illness—you have to maintain your equanimity. This is the central teaching of the Gita. The lotus is in the water, but not touched by it. So are you *in* life but you should not be *of* it," says Mohan.

So, does this philosophy work in the real world to help Hindus deal with the biggest loss of all? "I think it does a pretty good job of helping them handle their own death, but not the death of a loved one," says Dr. Mohan. "In spite of all that is taught about the transitoriness of life, and impermanence, and everyone has their own journey, and all that—Hindus are very attached."

Perhaps the doctrine of a people preaches the very thing that they need to work on most. Mohan, who has taught philosophy and religious studies for several decades, points to the great thinkers of Greek antiquity and their great exhortations about the value of moderation. "The truth of the matter is, these people were not so wonderfully moderate—they were so bloody contentious, so acquisitive, so violent. Naturally you have to teach the virtue of moderation to people who exhibit such extremes," he says. So, he theorizes, the doctrine of nonattachment is preached to Hindus because "they are so bloody attached to everything they have, and loss causes a big wrench in the emotions of these people."

By way of illustration, Mohan, who is a Brahman priest, says he once officiated at the cremation of a young man who was run over by a train. "He had just been married and the twenty-year-old bride was just beside herself with grief, and I didn't know the young man, but the whole scene was like the end of the world. I got all caught up in it and I couldn't even control myself to be able to perform the ceremony. It was just impossible."

A similar doctrine of impermanence is Buddhism's path to transcending all thoughts and emotions, as is the notion that there is no separate self or soul. All is one and all is illusion. Such a philosophy seems to help even those whose destinies are quite clearly written on their foreheads. Kobutsu Malone, a Zen priest with a prison practice that includes death row chaplaincy, says that many of his men say that their Zen practice gives them peace and dignity. Kobutsu believes Zen is the only thing that keeps them from "going off the deep end." And does Zen allow him also to view this aspect of life with equanimity?

"I'm not a very good monk," Kobutsu confesses. "I'm not very good at being nonattached. Four years ago I witnessed the execution of one of my men. I was profoundly affected. We had developed a really strong friendship and it was very much like watching someone kill my brother." Similarly, he says, "In the big picture, a starving child in Africa is nothing. But when you're holding that starving child in your arms—that child is the universe." How can this be? "We're still human beings—we do have to recognize our humanity. As much as you want to tell me we are nothing—that's not going to help me when I'm standing there with my child who is injured or dead. My reality is yes, I do form attachments . . . to my kids, my friends . . . these are people I choose to love and care about. As Professor Mohan and Reverend Kobutsu show, irrepressible humanity and heartfelt compassion save Eastern religions from a doctrine of passivity and a cold detachment that would do nothing to alleviate suffering and promote joy in the world.

RHYTHMS OF MOURNING

No matter why losses occur, we need to properly mourn our losses, and for most people loss of a loved one is the hardest blow of all. Death is a vacuum that sucks the joy and life out of the survivors. It brings chaos, uncertainty and instability; even when the death is "expected" it is a shock to the system. To calm the chaos and soothe our souls we have a tremendous need for the type of structure and stability offered by religious ritual.

All religious traditions have rituals that guide us along the long and winding road of mourning and saying goodbye. We must especially admire the set series of rites and observances that were developed over 2,000 years ago by ancient Jews. They knew then what modern psychology has only recently discovered: you can't hurry through "grief work," the step-by-step process that eventually allows us to heal and get on with life. So it is also with other losses in life. "Each bad thing is like a little death," points out Reverend Sharon Blackburn; "life is full of deaths." The Jewish way of grieving is a wonderful model that acknowledges the metaphysical side of death and mourning while addressing the practical and psychological aspects as well.

The traditional Jewish ritual consists of formal mourning periods of diminishing intensity. As Rabbi Ungar explains, "Death is a horrible thing!" But in observing the Jewish rituals of mourning "we move from sadness to joy by observing certain rituals and refraining from certain acts over a period of time. As time goes on, and grieving becomes less intense, more and more activities are gradually allowed."

Immediately upon the death of a Jewish person someone throws open the windows of the deceased's house to symbolically let the soul out and find its way up to God. Thus begins the first period of mourning: the *aninut*, a Hebrew word meaning "deep sorrow," is a legal category of mourning designating the time between death and burial. This is a time when the shock and grief are so great that you are allowed to weep, be in denial, be unreasonable, be angry, and say whatever you need to—but this should last no longer than three days.

At the funeral service, the mourners tear a garment as a symbol of their shredded and stricken spirits. The eulogy and other remembrances are spoken which, in the words of the Rabbi Margaret Holub, "fix, like fixer in a darkroom, an image of the life which blew through the universe like a comet." Then comes "the beautiful brutal custom of having family members pitch dirt into the grave," the hollow sound of which makes death real, writes Holub in Ornstein's *Lifecycles*.

The funeral is followed by the seven-day period of intense mourning called *shivah*, which means "seven." While sitting shivah, you are not expected to leave home, go to work or do any ordinary things such as bathe or have sex. Friends visit to bring food and express sympathy and talk about and remember the deceased. This period shelters and comforts the mourner. It allows you to grieve openly in the loving, caring inner sanctum closest to you, and frees you from the pressures of normal social and business activities and the need to put up a front for the outside world. Shivah is the buffer time between the death and the slow journey back to normal activities. At the end of shivah, you walk around the block to signify your reentry to the outside world.

After shivah comes *sheloshim*. Sheloshim is a Hebrew word meaning "thirty" (referring to the traditional thirty-day period of mourning following burial) and actually includes the seven days of shivah, but more generally refers to the period of twenty-three days of less intense mourning following shivah. The mourner may leave the house and return to work—but dancing, listening to music and attending festive occasions are out, because these are inappropriate to mourning. There are other restrictions as well. After the sheloshim, the formal mourning period is over, unless your parent has died. In that case, for the next ten months, you still limit party going. You also regularly recite the *Kaddish*, a special prayer that expresses your faith in God in spite of your grief. The Kaddish is "word-music" that has a "hypnotic power," writes Herman Wouk in *This Is My God*. "The mourner who speaks it feels an instinctive solace and release . . . as though for the moment he is stretching his hand to the far shore and touching the hand of his departed."

At the twelfth month, the first anniversary of the loved one's death, you light a candle symbolizing the soul of the deceased. This first *yahrzeit* ("year's time") is a crucial part of the mourning process because it officially ends the mourning period. It gives everyone closure—it is time to sew up the torn garment. This doesn't mean you forget the deceased. But it does mean that you can close this chapter and get on with life, which is probably what your loved one would want you to do. At this point it is traditional to also dedicate the tombstone, which is a concrete symbol of the finality of it all. Thereafter, lighting the yahrzeit candle, reciting the Kaddish and visiting the grave become a part of the rhythm of remembrance. Rabbi Leon Klenicki says, "You must mourn thoroughly to break this particular cycle of sadness . . . to openly and freely mourn helps enormously with your inner healing, and the healing of the family. If you don't do it now, you'll never be finished and it will come back to haunt you."

Judaism's set mourning ritual gives you the time and space you need to grieve fully and to cope with a devastating loss. Most religions have a framework and some sort of timetable to follow and these templates can be very useful. They take the strain off those on whose shoulders the responsibility for making the arrangements usually fall—the very people who are also usually the most grief-stricken. But the one-size-fits-all approach can also be a cold and mechanical experience. So, these traditional ways of coping work for many people—but of course, not for everyone.

Rabbi Margaret Holub has noticed that people may not want to observe traditional mourning ritual. She negotiates with them to comply because "I sense the task of mourning may demand something different than what people want in the moment, may in fact be exactly the opposite of what they want. And there may be more at stake than they can possibly know in those early days of grief," she writes in *Lifecycles*. Still, she says, you must trust a "brilliant system of healing developed over millennia" and the wisdom of your own heart; and perhaps substitute the notion of "permitted" where tradition says "required" and "exempt" where it says "forbidden."

Sometimes a hybrid ceremony is most appropriate, and can bring people closer together who might otherwise be worlds apart. Rachel, who is Jewish and runs her own business near San Diego, recalls the recent death of her best friend's sixteen-year-old daughter, in a senseless car accident. "I was so angry at God. I went out into our yard one night and screamed at God, asking him why did he let this happen?" They finally buried the child's ashes a year after the cremation, because Rachel says it took that long for them to be able to deal with the grief. "We helped each other get through the crisis. My friend is a wicca and she ritualistically burned tobacco and drew circles. I said the Kaddish. It just seemed to work; it felt right. At the end, we both looked at each other and said, 'That was pretty cool.' It actually brought us closer together."

"Grief is not only a psychological response to a mystery. It is part of the mystery itself. Mourning is an essential process of *tikkun* (repair) by which the world can continue to function," writes Holub. Psychiatry tells us that people feel guilty when they hurry through funeral rites or come out of mourning too soon. We have simplified or even omitted many practices. For example, its impossible to hold a wake in a hospital or in today's tiny apartments. By choice, as one observer points out, we have progressed from providing "mourning clothes in twenty-four hours" to "twenty-four-hour mourning." We go back to work a day or two after the funeral and we commend people for "bearing up" so well. The dead are not only dead but they are forgotten, along with the other dead in the quicksand of anonymity. So it is with other major (and minor) losses in life. We don't recognize or acknowledge the true impact, so we bury our distress along with the memory, much too eagerly.

CYCLES OF CELEBRATION

No matter what our religious beliefs, we have plenty to celebrate—births, weddings, spring, harvest. All religions have formal set holidays that are times of cheer. Both Judaism and Christianity have major holy days full of joy that are nevertheless dipped in sadness and suffering. Like the Jewish way of mourning, they are deliberately designed to take us on a cyclic journey through sadness that ends in celebration.

Passover distills the essence of the Jewish soul, which has had thousands of years to develop its ability to both soar to the great heights of joys and sink to the depths of despair. Passover or

Pesach commemorates the departure, or Exodus of the Israelites, from Egypt and their escape from oppression and enslavement. The theme of Passover is exile and redemption, freedom from slavery, and it leaves one with a feeling of hope, not despair. "At Passover we feel sad and happy at the same time," observes Rabbi Klenicki. "We are sad at the slavery our people suffered, and happy at their liberation." Passover is celebrated in the month of Nisan, the month of miracles. It is no accident that Passover occurs in the spring, because this season echoes Israel's rebirth and regeneration.

The seder is the Passover meal of special foods and other customs related to the Exodus. A seder begins with everyone saying, "Let all who are hungry come and eat." But this holiday is not just about eating. An integral part of a seder is the reading of the *Haggadah*, a set of questions and answers that recreate the story of Exodus. It allows each Jew to feel that he or she has personally experienced the horror of slavery and the joy of the Exodus and to express thanks for his or her freedom. And it empowers him or her to pass on the gift of freedom to others. Passover continues to have deep meaning for the Jewish people and has been observed by oppressed Jews all over the world, even during the Spanish Inquisition, and even in Hitler's concentration camps. It is also a reminder that ethically Jews cannot enslave, degrade, torture or oppress other people in any way, and must work to free those who are enslaved by others.

Sukkot, on the other hand, is pure joy. In fact, it is known as the Festival of Joy, the Festival of Booths, or *Zeman Simchatenu* (the Season of Our Rejoicing) because it celebrates and gives thanks for a bountiful fall harvest and commemorates the forty years of Jewish wandering in the desert after Sinai, living in temporary tent-like structures or booths called sukkot. Regardless of the climate, observant Jews build their own version of a sukkah to re-experience the Exodus and remind them of God's command from the Book of Leviticus: "You shall dwell in booths for seven days . . . that your generations may know that I made the Children of Israel to dwell in booths, when I brought them out of the land of Egypt."

The booth is festooned with plants—fruits and vegetables, cornstalks and palm fronds—and sometimes with other decorations such as paper chains, origami ornaments or dolls from around the world. Weather permitting, the family eats and sleeps in this temporary shelter for the weeklong celebration; this practice is meant to provide continuity with the past by emulating the experiences of their ancestors. The sukkah instills joy and inspires contemplation. Sitting in the beautiful, exuberant but temporary shelter, one is reminded of the fleeting qualities of fruits, vegetables, friends, relatives . . . the bounty of the harvest is short-lived, and freedom is fragile if not guarded.

Purim is also a happy holiday, but tinged with sadness. It is based on a story in the book of Esther in which the Jews were slated for extermination, but on the day of execution, their executioner suddenly died. So instead of a day of death and mourning, the day that dawned was one of joy and celebration. In celebrating Purim, the tactic is oblivion: children and adults alike get to dress up in silly costumes, abandon themselves and play games. The Talmud obligates each adult to be so drunk they can't tell the difference between the villain and the hero. But the centerpiece of the synagogue service is the reading of the *Megillah*, the handwritten scrolling of the book of Esther. Every time the evil executioner is named, the congregation yells and tries to drown out the name of the evil one with stomping and noisemakers.

Easter, the centerpiece of the Christian faith and calendar, is a bittersweet attempt to integrate mourning and celebration. This holiday, along with the Holy Week preceding, is the occasion to remember the conception and mourn the betrayal, agony, crucifixion and death of Jesus, and to celebrate the miracle of his resurrection. The life and meaning of Jesus is at the heart of the Christian creed and more than anything is what sets this religion apart form Judaism and Islam. "From the moments of great joy to the moments of utter despair, he is the ultimate model for us in every single aspect of our lives," says Tedeschi. "We venerate his suffering on the cross because it is the symbol of our own suffering and our own reconciliation with God. It is the symbol of ultimate obedience and courage. Remember, Jesus could have done something else." In fact, at one point, Jesus did get down on his knees and pray for God to let him out of his commitment. And on the cross, he cried "God, why have you forsaken me?" This, Christians say, proved Jesus' humanity.

"Jesus experienced everything we experience, right up to his death," says Tedeschi. "And the resurrection that lies beyond it. That is our model and our path." It is the overriding theme of hope that is the big message of Easter, and for the devout it can be an annual catharsis, a renewal. The liturgy of Lenten and Easter services is designed to enhance this effect. Peter Stoltzfus notes that for the forty days of Lent that precede Easter Sunday, Christians do not speak or sing the word Alleluia.

> This creates a tension that we don't release until Easter Sunday. You defer that joyful response, so when you finally arrive at Easter, you feel you have been on this journey together and that things are made right again by the Easter celebration.

But is a once-yearly catharsis enough? Robert Cormier, a Catholic priest in New Jersey, points out that although his faith offers Easter and Holy Week as a cyclical event that helps people deal with loss, we also need a weekly cycle for restoration because we have many little losses throughout the year. That's why "every Sunday is a little Easter. And the resurrection is why funerals are thought of as 'celebrations'—death is an entry to a better world and that person's life here and in the next life are celebrated."

UNFINISHED BUSINESS

Some people ask, what if God purposely did not complete the act of creation, but wants us to take a creative role in its unfolding? What if God considers this imperfect life, this universe to be a collaborative effort, an effort in which He is right here beside us when we feel either heart-bursting joy or heart-breaking pain? What if He suffers when we suffer and rejoices when we rejoice? What if humanity suffers and rejoices together, on a micro and macro level? Is life at least in part literally what we make of it?

Can we, through experiencing the big and little joys and sorrows of life, feel closer to God and to each other? The experiences are exactly what enable us to express who we are at that moment, and to find out who our God is. Good and bad luck alike give us a chance to be good Christians, Jews, Muslims, Hindus, Buddhists and human beings. When fortune smiles, do we celebrate our blessings? Are we gracious and modest and thankful? Do we share them and our delight in them? When bad luck strikes do we fully mourn our losses, learn from them and accept the help of others to lighten our burden? How do we help others in their times of need? Are we envious when we feel they are more fortunate than we are? Do the vicissitudes of life make us more aware of being alive, of being conscious, sentient beings and the only species that asks, "Why?"

When some wonderful thing happens, we may cast our eyes heavenward and utter a brief, "Thank you, God." But many of us pray only when adversity presents itself. And what should we pray for? "I am a praying man," writes Wayne Dosick in *When Life Hurts*. But when he heard that his home was in danger of being lost in a conflagration in the San Diego Hills, even this rabbi admits, "I had trouble praying," because he knows that prayer cannot change reality. So he could not pray that his home was not in the fire. If his home was destroyed, he couldn't pray that he and his family would not be spared anguish and pain, since it is human to feel these things.

> So I prayed the best I could, for the wisdom and the strength to face whatever lay before me—to feel true gratitude and deep joy if our house had been spared; to act with courage and dignity if our house were gone.

When he found out that his house indeed was gone, he prayed that God would be with him, to help him and give him some of His strength and courage, insight, wisdom, fortitude, counsel, guidance, understanding, caring, compassion and love, because "I cannot do this alone." And he found that "God is right beside me, right with me, right within me." Dosick says we can choose how we cope—*Redzech en* in Yiddish, means to "talk yourself into it" and that's how we cope.

Harold Kushner writes, "Prayer, when it is offered in the right way, redeems people from isolation. It assures them that they need not feel alone and abandoned. It lets them know that they are a part of a larger reality, with more depth, more hope, more courage, and more of a future than any individual could have by himself." Prayer puts us in touch with God, yes, but Kushner points out that "prayer puts us in touch with other people, people who share the same concerns, values, dreams and pains that we do."

Pain and pleasure, mourning and celebration seem to be not about us as individuals, but about us as people. Dosick is one of many disaster victims to have been touched by the gifts from the hearts and hands of family, neighbors, friends and even perfect strangers. One of the most strangely moving stories he tells is that of the stranger who came up to him while he was sifting through the ashes of his life. She handed him a plastic bag filled with ice, two cans of root beer and two peanut butter cups. She explained that her house had burned down in the Oakland Hills fire about five years earlier and a stranger had come up to her with two cans of root beer and two peanut butter cups. She said, "Even in the horror of that moment, it made me smile and feel a little better." She came to return the favor and hoped that her gift made him feel a little better too. In this sweet, thoughtful, creative, idiosyncratic human response we can rejoice. Each hardship provides a singular opportunity for other people to reveal their true stripes and rise to the occasion by showing understanding and compassion, and by giving of themselves.

As Tedeschi says, "We are all bound together. We are responsible for helping each other, in the life of prayer and active work. We are called upon to be stewards of each other, and of the earth." All of life's experiences allow God to shine through in yourself and in the people who emerge to help you, comfort you and just keep you company. Can we be present, through good times and bad, for ourselves and for other people? Can we be aware of God's presence and the goodness of human-ity, in whatever form they take, be it through bread and wine—or two cans of root beer and two peanut butter cups?

8. *Youth and Maturity*

> *Compareth the age of man unto the foure seasons of the yeare: the tyme that he groweth, is like the spring; the tyme of his strength, is like the sommer; the tyme that he beginneth to be wise, is like the harvest; and his age is like wynter, which finisheth all things.*
>
> —John Florio, *Firste Fruites*

> *The body advances while the mind flutters around it like a bird.*
>
> —Jules Renard, *Journal*

Consider the caterpillar. Once it reaches a certain age and size, it knows just what to do. It forms a protective shell and suspends itself from a twig on a tiny silk pad. Inside the shell, it undergoes a metamorphosis that is precisely prescribed by Nature. Its body changes and it forms beautiful, delicate wings, colored with all the hues of the rainbow. When it reaches maturity, it breaks out of its shell and voilà: a butterfly.

If only life's transitions were that clear, that simple, for us humans. But they are not. And our religious traditions know it; that's why rites of passage, or life-cycle rituals, exist.

Throughout history, we have needed rituals to shepherd us

through the confusing, awesome, lonely and otherwise chaotic, shapeless journey of our lifetimes. We've needed them to mark our passage from one stage of life to the next, one role to the next. We've needed the "endless rich ceremony" that cultures have devised "to help us engage the loss of the old and to give us courage to embrace what is new," writes Getrud Nelson in *To Dance With God.* We need rituals to announce our birth to the world, to initiate us into our religions, to usher us into adulthood and to marriage, and we need rituals to say goodbye to life.

Back in the days when the world was a tribal place, the demarcations between these stages were delightfully dramatic. You were a child. You were initiated into the tribe. You were married. You became a parent. You died. At each stage, thanks to ritual ceremony, there was a distinct transformation. There was no waffling. Although the physical process of maturation proceeded at its own more leisurely pace, socially, we were more like the caterpillar: when it was time, it was time. Your social, economic and spiritual self changed in cooperation with your irrevocably changed biological self. There was no going back and reverting to your former self, your former ways.

Making the transition from one life stage to the next was difficult and frightening enough in the past. Today, we belong to many groups or tribes, networks or communities. We get married, unmarried, remarried or not married at all. We move from place to place, country to country and job to job; our economic status skyrockets or plunges with the stockmarket; our elderly experience a second life after retirement and death is often a long-drawn dragged out affair. When you add up all the layers of being that characterize life in today's technologically developed countries, it's no wonder we have trouble answering the simple questions: Who am I? What am I? Where am I going? Am I there yet?

At the same time, religious life-cycle rituals—the very events that helped us answer those questions in previous generations—have faded from our lives. We are bored by them and cynical about them. We have lost their true meaning. We skip them, have no time for them or just go through the motions as we get all caught up in throwing expensive, status-conscious, ostentatious and overblown parties for the big occasion— mistaking money for meaning and materialism for substance.

This sorry state of affairs has not gone unnoticed by religious leaders or by the mental health profession. David Maybury-Lewis writes, "The generations no longer tell each other what makes an identity, institutions tells us. And they don't care. We, and especially the young, are isolated in a wide, empty plain. From afar it looks like freedom. But from where you stand, it looks like being lost."

This is not just the older generation bemoaning a golden past, a lost way of life. Researchers have made some distressing connections between many of our social ills and a lack of ritual in general and in coming-of-age-rituals in particular. For example, Dr. William Quinn, director of the Marriage and Family Therapy Program at Texas Tech University, and colleagues have written that "culturally defined and accepted rites of passage" have "given way to a more vague meaningless set of adolescent expectations and affirmations." As a result, on the one hand we have the "hurried child" who is expected to be more self-sufficient than is reasonable, and on the other hand, we have teenagers going through a prolonged dependence in which they demand to be treated as adults but still behave like children. No one is happy with the confusion and power struggle that inevitably ensues.

Young people also need the comforting little rituals—family prayer, communion, weekly services—the tiny rhythms of life that lead up to or flow out of the major life-cycle extravaganzas. According to Dr. Bette Keltner and her colleagues at the

Department of Nursing at California State University, family routines provide teens with the stability, dependability and intimate relationships that are generally lacking in families of problem teens. Divorce, remarriage, two working parents and so on have caused many of these "anchor-producing practices" to fall by the wayside.

Nature abhors a vacuum, and kids will always try to fill the gap as best they know how. Dr. Saul Levine and Nancy Salter of the University of Toronto investigated the appeal of mystical new religious groups and cults to young people. They found that the most common reasons given were feelings of loneliness, rejection, sadness, feelings of not belonging anywhere, lack of meaning and the need for a mystical experience or dimension to their lives. These authors observed that the diminishing role of rituals in North America "is keenly felt by our youth." They point out that Orthodox religions have, by and large "been unresponsive and irrelevant to the spiritual needs of young people."

More and more, the non-Orthodox religions are listening, however, and realize that because times change, cultures change; therefore needs change, and our religious rites need to change, too. All religious traditions and their rituals need to evolve if a religion is to stay alive, but life-cycle rites exist in a special world of exquisite tension and conflict, where they collide with heated debates about what it means to be human; about the cult of the individual versus the need to be part of a group; about nature versus nurture and what it means to be a man or a woman; about who can get married (and unmarried) and about the participation of the laity in rituals.

For example, Judaism and Christianity have responded by making marriage ceremonies more equitable and celebrated with two rings, not just one. After Vatican II, Roman Catholic rites became simplified and their symbolism clearer; they were celebrated in the vernacular, not Latin, and they became more communal and emphasized the participation of the laity. The rabbis of Reform Judaism created quite a stir when they agreed to recognize same-sex marriages. Judaism now celebrates not only a boy's coming of age (bar mitzvah), but also a girl's coming of age (bat mitzvah) publicly.

Rites-of-passage ceremonies and the thinking behind them are often intertwined with our fundamental notions of social and cultural identity. Since our notions of self, community and personal identity in relation to religion are changing, how we "practice" our faith is changing as well. For example, certain local customs that have nothing to do with Islam are falling by the wayside, particularly those relating to marriage and circumcision.

These and other changes need to be made to keep life-cycle rituals relevant but they need to be done cautiously and delicately. Debra Orenstein, who is critical of the more Orthodox Jewish tradition rituals, has edited a book, *Life Cycles: Jewish Women on Life Passages and Personal Milestones.* It is a collection of the views of feminists who are addressing the lack of attention, opportunity and education that women have suffered throughout the history of Judaism. It calls attention to inequities in traditional Jewish practices that are a reflection of the notion that only men are linked to the mind and God, and women are linked to the earth and body.

Traditional rites of passage were created to meet a variety of needs, and they continue to do so. They instill in us the values of the religious community, make us feel part of a continuous history and reassure us that life and our stages in it have meaning and purpose. They fulfill our need to be acknowledged by our community, our need for bonding and a sense of belonging. They create structures that provide some predictability and safety around times in our lives when we suffer insecurity, transition or loss, says Orenstein. They also offer the physical signs of the inner transformation—the invisible and ineffable made tangible and real.

That's why even the "most progressive feminists are cautious about making changes," writes Orenstein. "We have great attachments to and nostalgia for the Jewish wedding ceremony as a whole. The *Sheva Berakhot* (seven marital blessings) are breathtakingly beautiful and, except for masculine God language, completely non-sexist." Even "politically incorrect" aspects of the wedding may be quite moving, she feels, and gives as an example the traditional marriage contract, which is not a mutual document, but which she values "for the antiquity of the language, the continuity of its usage, the artwork and calligraphy that it has inspired over the centuries, and the fact of its acceptance by all segments of the Jewish community."

Long before psychology was invented, wise people knew the value of symbolism and action, of ceremonially letting go of our old familiar selves and embracing our new, unfamiliar selves. It seems foolish to toss away this ancient wisdom and traditional ritual completely—to throw the baby out with the baptismal water. But it seems also unwise to continue to slavishly follow outmoded ways of thinking, as if we were living in a time capsule on a deserted island. Transitional rituals themselves now need to take some of their own medicine—to let go of some aspects of the past, breathe new life into others, and learn to integrate them with the present. Our old transitional rituals themselves are in a painful stage of transition, locked in a struggle, as Rav Kuk says, of the "renewal of the old and the sanctification of the new."

SAMSKARA, MITZVOT, SACRAMENTS

By definition, life-cycle rites span a lifetime, but the rituals religion deems most important relate to marriage and the assumed procreation that follows. In spite of the centrality of making babies, the rites pay far more attention to males than to females, who are secondary characters in the cultures from which the major traditions sprang. Another universal theme in these rites of passage is purification—and women become ritually unclean far more often than men do, usually through their role in reproduction. More than any other rituals, those related to the life cycle are heavily flavored by local customs, which tend to be paternalistic.

Hindus have perhaps the most highly developed system of rites of passage, called *samskara*. Historically there were as many as forty samskaras or more, but in modern Hinduism, "only" ten to eighteen are practiced (childhood samskaras are performed only within the upper class), with only two practiced regularly: the marriage and the funeral. Samskaras prepare a person for his or her new place in the world by imparting new qualities or removing impurities, or both. They are usually quite elaborate affairs, and begin with conception. By the numbers, most rites are childhood rites; however, as is typical in most cultures, the central Hindu institution is marriage. All other samskaras either lead up to marriage or flow out of it. Judaism also has a highly developed series of rites that usher the person through life. Jewish rites are generally rooted in the Bible and are called *mitzvot* or "commandments." The overall purpose of Jewish life-cycle rites is to permit the individual and the community to experience the changing status of their relationships.

In Christianity, life-cycle rites may also be *sacraments*. Sacraments were the acts of Christ; they bestowed "grace," a phenomenon that elevates the human spirit, gives it access to an intimate union with the Divine and leads to salvation. The Catholic Church recognizes seven such sacraments: baptism, the Eucharist, confirmation, penance, marriage, ordination into the church and extreme unction. Most Protestant churches recognize only baptism and the Eucharist because there is no evidence the other rites were ordained by Christ.

Islam itself is not enamored of rites in general. It is a rather austere, no frills religion and the usual rites of passage are not specific to Islam. Marriage, for example, is a secular contract. Because of the breathtaking diversity of cultures that practice Islam, rites tend to be shaped by local custom and have been tolerated as long as they do not directly contradict the universal aspects of Islam. This appears to be changing, however, as modernist Muslim sentiment against some of these impure customs intensifies.

BIRTH & CHILDHOOD: WELCOME & INITIATION

Is there anything sweeter, more vulnerable and more miraculous than a new baby? What does this amazing creature need? It needs to be announced and welcomed into the world. It needs to be named and, in some traditions, it needs to be initiated immediately into the religion of its parents. All religions rejoice at the birth of a baby and want to keep this miracle of life safe from harm so it will survive and fulfill its mission in the tradition.

Hinduism probably wins the prize for the highest number of birth and childhood rituals. Rituals begin before birth and aim to ensure conception and the health of the mother and the fetus. The largest number of samskaras occurs between birth and adolescence because this was the most precarious time of life in premodern societies. As Rachel McDermott puts it, "You needed a lot of ritual to protect them from dying." Certain rites must be performed immediately after birth, when it is paramount that the father hold the baby and whisper a protective mantra in its ear. The naming ceremony occurs on the tenth or twelfth day after birth. Other rites mark the first solid food eaten by the baby, having her or his ears pierced and the first haircut.

Dr. Anand Mohan, who was born into the Brahman caste, describes a childhood ritual unique to Hinduism. "Things are put in front of the child, such as toys, gold, certain types of food.

The relatives then watch to see what the child will grab," as an indication of the child's tendencies. "The relatives yell and scream, trying to influence the child to grab certain things. The baby also picks the main deity he or she wants to worship—the goddess of learning, the goddess of money and so on." His parents were dismayed when young Amand chose the goddess of learning, "and that's probably why to this day, I am teaching at Queens College and have little money," he says.

Among the Dagara people of South Africa, a child is a special treasure, and treated as such. Malidoma Patrice Somé tells why in his beautiful little book *Ritual: Power Healing, and Community*. It speaks volumes about the Dagara worldview and the unfolding of the life cycle. Somé writes:

> The first few years of life of a male child are spent with the grandfather. There is an unspoken closeness between one who has freshly entered from the other world and one who is close to returning to the other world. Grandfathers want to know as much as possible about the state of affairs on the other side before returning. And the children will slowly grow into forgetting the grandness of the realm they came from.

Although children are intensely loved, Judaism has the most controversial and painful rite for a newborn baby boy: circumcision. This ritual is performed at home, and is called *berit milah* ("covenant of circumcision"). It involves surgically removing the foreskin of the penis and tearing off and folding back the mucus membrane to expose the glands. This is performed on the baby's eighth day of life because that is the completion of the child's first cycle, a period of a week. It is performed by a *mohel*, a specially trained circumciser. The baby is either placed on a restraining board or, more generally, the father holds down his legs. After the surgery, which is performed without anesthesia, the child is given a little wine.

Modern Judaism is not alone in the rite of circumcision. This ancient practice of many Near Eastern cultures was probably observed as a fertility rite. Ancient pagan tribes sacrificed their firstborn male children, with the idea that if the gods were satisfied they would allow their subsequent sons to live long and full lives. Some historians believe that this human sacrifice evolved into the symbolic sacrifice of circumcision. In any event, Judaism adapted this common folk ritual and gave it new meaning. Among Jews circumcision became the physical sign of belonging to the Jewish people or nation and in the Jewish Bible, God says to Abraham: "You shall circumcise the flesh of your foreskin, and that shall be the sign of the covenant between me and you. And throughout the generations, every male among you shall be circumcised at the age of eight days. Thus shall my covenant be marked in your flesh as an everlasting pact."

Rabbi Irvin Ungar has a son and has conducted many *berit milahs*. He admits, "This is a great moment of fear, too. You are proud of your son, but you are also hoping you selected the right mohel. You are worried that your kid will cry. The mother usually doesn't watch. The father usually pretends to watch while he is thinking that the mohel shouldn't cut too much." He feels this ceremony has intangible benefits beyond the significance of the covenant. It "brings parents even closer together. You're not just focussing on your child coming into the community, but you also feel proud of what you did, what you made, as if it's never happened to anyone else. And in a sense, it hasn't."

As is the case with *kashrut*, the dietary restrictions kept by kosher Jews, attempts have been made to justify circumcision on medical or health grounds. Studies purported to prove its health benefits do not hold up. It has also been claimed that the baby is too young to feel any pain. This, too, has been disproved. A chilling new study by the Natural Institutes of Health suggests that even premature babies are not only capable of feeling pain, but that the pain of surgery causes more nerves to grow in the area, leaving the baby permanently hypersensitive to pain as it grows older. Even so, Jewish parents continue to practice circumcision, often out of a combination of fear that their son would otherwise feel different from the other lads at school, or because of the powerful message that, as Herman Wouk puts it "circumcision is the old seal of the pledge between Abraham and his creator, a sign in the flesh, a mark at the source of life." Rabbi Leon Klenicki says the circumcision "gives the boy a Jewish commitment, and it gives the boy the anatomy that matches those of other Jewish boys. I've known uncircumcised older boys who decided on their own to undergo circumcision at a later age, which is a much more serious operation." However this Jewish commitment to the covenant by sign of the flesh doesn't explain why Muslims and so many Christians also circumcise their boys.

Infant girls traditionally get their names during a ceremony in the synagogue—not in the home, as with boys—within thirty days of their birth but there is no surgical counterpart to circumcision. (Thank goodness: this is one type of equality no one needs.) Reform Judaism adopted a new rite called *berit ha-hayyim* ("covenant of life"). It follows the same liturgy as berit milah and involves lighting candles and saying blessings. Other non-Orthodox synagogues have followed suit.

Among certain societies, including those of many Islamic countries, females are also "circumcised"—the accurate term is clitoridectomy—which includes cutting away all or part of the external genitalia, including the exquisitely sensitive clitoris. This practice is done for psychosexual and religious reasons, and adherents claim it increases fertility, promotes hygiene and strengthens social cohesiveness. However, in reality it can cause women agonizing pain during urination, sexual intercourse and childbirth, as well as lead to infection and death. Each year two million women (actually, infants, young girls, teenagers and women) are at risk of joining the already 140 million women the World Health Organization estimates have undergone the procedure.

Naming the baby is another important component of the life-cycle ritual. "Judaism teaches that one's name can influence one's personality," says Irvin Ungar. It is customary to name a Jewish child after a relative who is deceased, as a way to memorialize them and keep their spirit alive. Ungar named his son Raziel Chayam, after his mother; he gave him the middle name Adam. Ungar says Raziel is also "the name of the angel who appeared to Adam in the Garden of Eden and gave him a book containing all the divine secrets about the mystery of creation." With all that legend and lore behind it, Raziel was inspired to write his college essay about his name.

Baptism is Christianity's initiation-and-naming ritual. In an infant it represents a washing away of the sin he is born with; thus cleansed, he enters the Church and becomes a Christian. At the public ceremony, which takes place during a regular church service, the baby also gets his name, his "Christian" name. His Godparents promise that together with the parents they will see that the child grows up in the Christian faith. Seems simple enough, but baptism is not without its controversy—but on theological rather than ethical, medical or political grounds. Baptism is based on the story of Creation and Adam and Eve's "original sin"—the sin with which we are burdened at birth and which needs to be "washed away." This "born tainted" interpretation is hard to accept for some Christians.

Baptism is also based on the symbolism of water as a tool for spiritual cleansing and regeneration: the deluge which wiped the earth clean of sinners and degenerates, the passing through the waters of the Red Sea at the Exodus and Judaism's ritual purifying bath. In early Christianity, baptism was by total immersion, preferably in running water. Some denominations insist this is the only way to really wash away sin; the sprinkling that most babies receive is not sufficient. Furthermore, in some denominations, baptism is considered to be a rite of adulthood, because only adults can join the Church of their own free will.

Christian baptism gradually took the place of the Jewish rite of circumcision, as initiation into the religion, except it is a rite of female infants, too. Even if one is skeptical about the importance of original sin and the need to ritually wash it away as soon after birth as possible, there are those, such as Matthew Fox, who believe baptism is still an important religious ritual.

Fox writes in *Signs of the Spirit, Blessings of the Flesh*: "Baptism is a new beginning, it is a welcoming into this universe, into this particular time and place, into this particular community and family." Water, he points out, is a universal symbol for purity, and "something we hold in common with all living things." Because it relates us to the whole of nature, he says, "it is cosmic."

In Islamic cultures, the first word a baby should hear is "Allah," a word the father tenderly whispers into the child's ear. On the seventh day after the child's birth comes the naming and welcoming, said to be the most important day in the child's life. The most popular name for a boy is Muhammad, both in Arab and non-Arab countries. On this momentous day, little Muhammad tastes the sweetness of life: he gets a sweet food, such as honey, touched to his lips, and then relatives pass him from one to another, each one whispering a prayer into his ear. This signifies that the baby is part of the community and that all present are responsible for his well being—rather like an extended family of Godparents. Between the ages of two and seven, Muhammad gets circumcised, a ritual that prepares him to assume the religious responsibilities of an adult, including the five-times-a-day prayers and the Ramadan fast.

COMING OF AGE: CONFIRMATION & PARTICIPATION

Is there a time of life that is more frightening and challenging, more exciting and ambivalent than adolescence? Hormones raging, voice changing, breasts budding, penises swelling, pimples sprouting. Adulthood beckons, childhood clings, and you flicker between these two worlds in the blink of an eye. No wonder teens are unsure and confused. A coming-of-age-ceremony can address these emotions and help adolescents deal with them by giving them symbolic form. Confirmation, bat and bar mitzvah, upanayana—these initiation rites help usher the adolescent from a happy, carefree, familiar childhood to an unknown and thrillingly responsible adulthood.

Alas, the transformation doesn't happen overnight. At age fourteen, Elana Rosenfeld Berkowitz reminisces about her bat mitzvah in *Life Cycles*:

> It was frustrating to me that I could not in a flash of light have the meaning of my bat mitzvah revealed to me. Instead, I came to realize that public moments must be discrete in time while personal development continues. . . . While I feel that a spiritual turning point did not occur at my bat mizvah, it was certainly a significant ritual marker in my transition from child to woman. . . . My parents felt as I did, in that they saw my bat mitzvah as a link in a chain to God, rather than a monumental change.

We find initiation rituals in every major religion. In pre-industrial societies, it is often an ordeal—involving knocking out a tooth, scarification, tattooing, circumcision (without anesthetic), the wearing of unwieldy masks and costumes, and periods of separation, isolation, fasting and other tests of strength and tenacity. When rites are this intense and this emotional, it's not surprising the results are so dramatic—unlike Berkowitz's experience, when the initiate emerges from the process the child has symbolically died and feels reborn as an adult.

As might be expected, coming-of-age rites have a strong educational aspect—kids learn the history, ethics, morals and standards of their religious faith—which, their parents hope, will also guide them through life in the secular world.

In societies where religious tradition and cultural tradition form a seamless web, "puberty rites" introduce the child into the immediate world of spiritual and cultural values and make him or her a responsible member of society. In societies where religious traditions weave a web separate from the predominant culture this doesn't necessarily happen. Many of us live two lives and often our religious values clash with those of the secular world. Religious rituals such as confirmation and initiation tell us who we are and what is expected of us in the religious realm, but not necessarily the secular. This "double life" is a test of strength of character to be sure and one that does not occur in pre-industrial, all-one-web societies—although as they industrialize this dissonance is bound to affect them too.

In India's Hinduism, we see the remnants of the initiation ceremony (for boys only) of one such complete society. *Upanayana* is regarded as a "second birth" and is open to only the three upper social classes, who are also called "twice born." Depending on the class, boys from age eight to twelve participate in a rite that includes a special meal, a bath, a head shaving and the bestowing of a "sacred thread" worn over the left shoulder and under the right arm. During the ceremony, the boy's teacher performs symbolic acts that bind the two together. Traditionally, the boy would remain in his teacher's house, separated from the social community and his family, where he learns humility, obedience and chastity. At the end of this tutorial, the youth undergoes a rite called *samavartana*, which reincorporates

him into the adult world. The ceremony again involves a ritual
bath, after which he dons fine clothes, assumes his status in society and is ready to begin the search for a suitable bride. Dr.
Mohan says, "When girls reach a certain age, they have a ceremony in the house. It's basically an advertising gimmick,
announcing that the girl is of marriageable age."

In Judaism, the coming of age ritual for a boy is the *bar mitzvah* ("son of the commandment"). It is usually performed when
he is thirteen—the age at which he is considered mature enough
to grasp the concepts of Judaism and stable enough to hold to
the disciplines. For a girl it is the *bat mitzvah* ("daughter of the
commandment") and the traditional age is twelve. "This is a special moment at which a boy and girl realize their maturity. It is
a moment of great transformation," says Rabbi Klenicki.
However, bar and bat mitzvah, he observes, has become an
"American industry."

A year before the ceremony, the boy or girl and parents start
planning the large party that follows the ceremony. They carefully consider the guest list, the invitations, the food, the color
scheme and the music. They speculate on the gifts they will be
getting, and who will be giving cash and how much. They need
to find and schedule performers and musicians to entertain the
guests, who may arrive in limousines and be wearing the latest
fashions. Let's see; did we forget something?

Oy vay! They also have to prepare for the ceremony! The
boy will be studying the Torah so he will be able to recite it without too much embarrassment in front of the rapt congregation.
He will also be preparing the Sabbath service he will be leading
in the synagogue. And the girl? Traditionally, girls and women
are exempt from most Orthodox Jewish ritual and exempt from
advanced Hebrew studies. A woman's job is to care for her family so her husband can study the Jewish texts unencumbered by
mundane concerns. So, until recently, there was no public cere-

mony in the synagogue for her coming of age. No public reading from the Torah, no leading of prayers.

Fortunately, two important changes are underway. With no
official guidelines or rules, many women are creating their own
bat mitzvah rituals. Some resemble the bar mitzvah ceremony,
others come up with something unique. Even in Orthodox
Judaism, bat mitzvahs are beginning to have a public ritual component; some girls are leading prayers and chanting the Torah at
all-women's prayer groups; others are studying portions of the
texts and celebrating the accomplishment.

For her daughter's bat mitzvah, Jessica Gribetz enlisted the
assistance of an Israeli scholar and her sister Naomi. Together
they selected the stories of nine biblical women as examples of
insights and virtues to emulate, such as Sarah's patience,
Rebecca's vision, Miriam's music and Ruth's loyalty. Geribetz
writes in her book, *Wise Words* that they hoped that these women
and the words of her female relatives "would fortify her [daugh-
ter's] sense of belonging to the unbroken chorus of Jewish
women throughout time who take responsibility for their share
in the Torah and the community." Three of her nieces have also
used the same service and she says it looks like this is the beginning of a real family tradition.

The second change under way is that some people are
eschewing ostentatious parties and putting the "mitzvah" back in
bar and bat mitzvahs by taking to heart the motto of Judaism,
tikkun olam ("repair of the world"). Mitzvah means good acts, and
teens are giving their money gifts to nonprofit organizations,
organizing fund raising events, and collecting merchandise and
food and donating them to worthy causes. Rabbi Jeffrey K.
Salkin, author of a book about bar and bat mitzvahs, says, "Jewish
celebrations should celebrate Jewish values. The educational and
spiritual part of bar and bat mitzvah can extend beyond the final
hymn at the service. It can permeate the lives of our young, and

it can enrich what they take with them into the world."

Confirmation at age twelve or thirteen is the big coming-of-age ritual in the Christian faith. In the Catholic Church confirmation is preceded by the first Communion, at age seven, where little girls dress up in frilly white dresses and little boys wear suits. Confirmation is exactly that—a ritual confirmation and public affirmation of the child's baptismal covenant made on her behalf when she was too young to understand what was going on. Some have described confirmation as a "second baptism." As with the Jewish coming-of-age rituals, the child studies the Scriptures for a certain time before the actual ceremony, during which she verbally reaffirms her renunciation of evil and renews her commitment to Jesus Christ. Father Cormier explains that through "instruction and education, you are able to make a choice in life. What do you believe? What will you do with your faith? Now you have a moral framework against which you can measure your thoughts and behavior; you will make fewer mistakes and learn from them."

Many non-Orthodox Jewish synagogues have also added a confirmation ceremony for boys and girls. It takes place when they are sixteen or seventeen and is celebrated on Shavuot, the commemoration of the day the Jewish people received the Torah. As is the case with the Christian version of confirmation, this is an opportunity for older teens to affirm their commitment to their faith at an age at which they can better understand it.

MARRIAGE: PARTNERSHIP & PROCREATION

"Marriage—the ceremony among all ceremonies," beams Rabbi Ungar. "I remember my wedding," Unger recalls:

> watching my wife walking down the aisle, stepping up onto the platform. I remember thinking, "How beautiful she is." I

remember feeling like there was nothing else in the world at that moment, but also that there was *everything* else in the world. It felt so right. I felt connected to the first couple, to Adam and Eve, to the joy of creation itself.

Every culture, every religion recognizes some form of marriage. People marry for lots of religious and nonreligious reasons: it sanctions sexual activity and confers legitimacy to their children, as well as provides security and care for those children; it confers status and forms family, social and other alliances; it regulates line of descent and last but not least, it provides affection and companionship. Most people believe that men and women are not complete and cannot be happy until they have a spouse with whom to have children to initiate and pass on the family, cultural and religious tradition.

The religious purpose of marriage varies from tradition to tradition—some consider marriage to be a sacred act, a union of the souls or spirits. Judaism believes marriage is the ideal human relationship. Marriage was ordained by God, according to the book of Genesis, where God says: "It is not good for man to be alone; I will make a fitting helper for him . . . therefore shall a man . . . cleave unto his wife; and they shall be one flesh." The origin of the marriage custom is traced to Adam and Eve, the first marriage. Their union is part of the fabric of creation and therefore, so is any marriage. As Rabbi Ungar implies, marriage is a paradise regained, because man and woman are joined as they were in Eden.

Having put marriage on such a high pedestal, the Talmud (one-quarter of which deals with the relations between men and women) says that each happy pairing off is as difficult for the Almighty as the Parting of the Red Sea. Judaism believes that marriage is a blessing from God, a way to perpetuate the human race and to facilitate the couple's personal growth. It also con-

[handwritten margin note: except they weren't married!!]

siders marriage to be a legal, contractual relationship and therefore it may be dissolved through divorce.

Christianity likewise traces marriage to the original couple. The Christian wedding ceremony joins the bride and groom into one spirit, in union with God. Marriage is also a metaphor for the concept of the marriage of the Church to Christ—the bride and groom together become the "bride" of Christ. Catholics and Anglicans consider marriage to be a sacrament that conveys God's grace on the couple, a view not shared by Protestant denominations. In Islam, marriage is a secular contract, but it is also a divine covenant. Hinduism says that marriage is a sacred institution and the marriage ceremony unites the bride and groom into one spirit. Marriage is paramount in the grand scheme of things wherein only a man with a wife and male children can perform the required religious acts that repay his debts to his ancestors. Marriage also marks the arrival of adulthood for the Hindu woman, who otherwise has no coming-of-age rite of her own.

Economics also play a role in the ritual tying of the knot—the woman and her children must be supported. So, guests and family offer gifts, both real and symbolic. In Islam, the two families negotiate to set the size of the marriage payment. The payment indicates the value of the bride-to-be and is earmarked for domestic furnishings that remain the bride's property. No payment, no marriage by Islamic law. The wedding consists of the announcement of the dowry, an exchange of vows and signing of the agreement before witnesses. Judaism likewise has a legal contract, the *Ketubah*, which outlines responsibilities of each partner. The man is obligated to provide for his wife and satisfy her sexually; the woman is expected to honor her husband.

Most wedding ceremonies have a ritual that symbolizes the sacred union and rituals that are a foreshadowing of the marriage life to come. The couple may join hands, exchange rings or share a cup of wine. The Jewish ceremony takes place under a *chupah*, a canopy that symbolizes the couple's new relationship and the new home they will establish. The couple affirms their commitment, and seven beautiful blessings are chanted. In a Christian service, the bride and groom take each other's hands and exchange vows to love, comfort, cherish, honor and keep each other for better or worse, richer or poorer, in sickness and in health, and to be faithful to each other as long as they both shall live.

A Hindu wedding ceremony may last several hours and is conducted by a priest before a ceremonial fire in a wedding pavilion, built to symbolize the universe. The essential rite of the ceremony are the Seven Steps: the groom leads the bride to take seven steps to the northeast while he makes proclamations and invocations (of many sons and fertility), then together they walk around the sacred fire seven times. Buddhists have a civil—not a religious—ceremony but their weddings may include chanting from the Scriptures. Wedding ceremonies and the festivities after them can be modest or as elaborate as finances will allow.

Traditional wedding ceremonies of whichever faith tradition also incorporate fertility rites, no matter how disguised. These include, for example: displaying or tossing grains such as rice; having a small child, such as a flower girl, accompanying the bride; breaking an object or food. The most famous of the latter symbol occurs at the Jewish wedding when the groom smashes a glass by stomping on it. This is one of the highlights of the ceremony and everyone applauds and shouts "Mazel Tov" or best wishes. The breaking of the glass has been interpreted over the centuries to mean many things, but the talmudic origins of the practice reflected a symbolic breaking of the hymen. (A more modern reading of the practice is a warning that love, like glass is fragile and must be protected.) In any case, this also signals that it's time to party—the solemn mood changes in a flash. The music begins and the guests lift up the bride and groom who are sitting in chairs while the rest of the guests and family dance around them.

After the ceremony and the party—then what?

The liberal Jewish couple goes off on their honeymoon to the latest "in" resort.

The Christian couple goes off on their honeymoon during which they practice the rhythm method of birth control, if they are devout Catholics.

The Hindu couple goes to the husband's home, where they remain chaste for three days. Only after they perform fertility rites, may they consummate the marriage.

The Muslim couple leaves their guests; the husband enters the bridal chamber, lifts his bride's veil and offers her milk and dates before they consummate the marriage. The bride is confined to the home for one week. She can receive female visitors, but is forbidden to see her father, brothers and all male relatives for at least three months.

The Orthodox Jewish couple embarks on a life of alternating sexual abstinence and sexual activity. During her menstrual period and for the seven days after, sexual activity is forbidden, as a woman is considered to be ritually "unclean." Ritual uncleanliness means she is not allowed to participate in ritual observances—in the Orthodox worldview, the loss of blood and reproductive capacity means she cannot participate in rituals with a full and complete heart. So, for these twelve days of a woman's monthly cycle, in which the couple may not have sex, they sleep apart to avoid temptation (that's why twin beds are common in Orthodox households) and refrain from even touching or kissing each other. At the end of the twelve days, the woman takes a ritual bath at the community *mikveh*, a ritual pool built especially for symbolic ritual purification. After the bath, she and her husband resume sexual relations until her next period—approximately fifteen days.

This is almost the exact opposite of the rhythm method of

birth control—the couple abstains during the days a woman is least likely to conceive, and have intercourse on the days she is most fertile. This practice, called *taharat hamishpacha*, makes sense for couples who are interested in making as many Jewish babies as possible. However, it may be a cruel hardship for couples who love each other and love sex and would rather not limit their intimacy according to a schedule. On the other hand, some couples say imposing this on-again off-again rhythmic approach to intimacy has many benefits besides facilitating procreation. They say it keeps their marriages fresh and full of vitality. It gives each person his or her own space and private time. When they re-join on the twelfth day they are eager, passionate. Furthermore, it proves that they can control their animal passions and primitive instincts, elevates the relationship to a level of sacred holiness and deepens their commitment to each other and their marriage.

Orthodox Judaism is not alone in its attention to spiritual "purity." Hinduism has many rules and standards about purity and many purification rituals. When women are menstruating, they are not permitted to prepare food, according to Dr. Mohan. "They are put in an out-house building, and the men and boys have to cook for themselves," he says. In Islam, the new mother is also considered to be "ritually unclean" after giving birth, meaning she is not permitted to pray (or fast); she may be confined to the house for seven to forty days. After the confinement is over, female friends and relatives take her to the public bath to become purified so she may resume normal activities.

BETWEEN THE CRACKS

An alien visitor from another world looking at the life-cycle rituals of our developed countries would think that as humans we are born, we come of age, we marry, we die. Nothing significant happens afterward or in between. Even in cultures that venerate the elderly—where people recognize the last phase of life as important and worthy and take care of their elderly—there are no more rituals to speak of. All religions have funerals of course, but they don't count because we are not sure whether the dead are really present at these ceremonies, or whether they care what happens during them.

To find life-cycle rituals after marriage (except of course rituals which revolve around your children or grandchildren and which you may or may not be involved in) you really need to look around. In Southern India, Hindu men who reach their six-tieth birthday are honored with a big celebration. This birthday signals the third stage of life, the stage of contemplation says Dr. Mohan. "You can retreat from the hurly-burly of life—your children have grown up, your oldest son can take care of the family. If you want to, you can leave your life and really be a renunciate, shoot off to the hills."

In America, this is around the time our "seniors" retire to a life of endless golf. In Western cultures, some people may still have a retirement party. But this is rarely any longer at the company's expense, and there's probably no gold watch waiting for you either.

We live in a fragmented, confusing, complex, disorderly period of history. The Hindu name for it is *kali yuga*, the era of degeneration and chaos that precedes the end of the universe's present existence. Rachel McDermott says Hindus believe that "we need to do a lot of rituals and devotional practices in the present era because our world is so spritually degenerate." Pastor Cormier thinks the human spirit "has changed, so we need more rituals and support." Gertrud Nelson says,

> No moment of transition is too small or insignificant for the nourishment of rites or ceremony.

These are ways of saying that we need more meaningful rituals, not fewer ones. Precious moments in our lives are falling between the cracks. And we need to figure out ways to impart more meaning to the nonreligious occasions we do attempt to honor, both joyous and sad: childbirth, adoption, infertility, new jobs, miscarriage, abortion, first menstruation, divorce, empty nest, relocating to a new home, menopause. These can be "talked through" in social conversations with close friends and relatives, and in the therapist's office. But making it through these transitions requires more than a thinking brain. We are affected on all levels, so they must be approached on all levels, including the nonverbal levels, which rituals satisfy.

In our stubborn individuality we often go through transitions alone, in private. We entrust our lives and well being to strangers—"experts" who know only a part of our needs, and do not know us as people at all. People bare their souls and share the most sacred, emotional moments of their lives on "real" TV, and the audience laps it up, and participates. We are born in a hospital amidst the whirring, beeping and bright lights of technology. We come of age in the mall and learn to genuflect at the shrines of materialism. We marry (if at all) amidst status-obsessed splendor (maybe several times). And more likely than not, we die, as we are born, in a cold and lonely place, the swooshing and whispering of a nurse's night time perambulations the only audible prayer.

Where are our friends, our family, our ancestors' spirits to shepherd us through these important times? Frank Tedeschi reminds us that Christianity "is a community of faithful people." These ceremonies are important because, he says,

> They offer an individual the support of the community at critical moments in their lives. These ceremonies are all about relationship. They are mirrors and images of the divine rela-

tionship to itself and its creation, or our relationship to the creator and to each other. They are about love, which spills over to the creation. An infant is not baptized alone; it becomes part of something larger. The same holds true for confirmation and holy matrimony.

The world has changed since the days our ancestors designed our religious rituals, but basic human needs have not. Surely we deserve as much attention, support and love as our forebears did.

Ask any butterfly.

9. *Death and Beyond*

*Dance like no one's watching, love like you'll
never be hurt, sing like no one's listening,
live like it's heaven on earth.*

—William Pukey

*It's not that I'm afraid to die. I just don't want
to be there when it happens.*

—Woody Allen, Death (a play)

It's here, at last. The moment you've been waiting for. If your heart could beat, it would beat with fear. If your mind could think, it would burst with curiosity. If you had a soul, it would be getting ready to leave your body. Because, dear reader, this is the moment of your own death.

Perhaps you are in the comforting warmth and familiarity of your own home, a hospice worker tending to your needs, with family and friends watchful, tearful, holding your hand and murmuring sweet somethings in your ear. Perhaps you're on the gravely shoulder of a six-lane highway, the rain slicing down at a cruel forty-five-degree angle, your car totaled, your body man-

195

gled, with police lights blinking and some good Samaritan pumping madly at your unresponsive chest, blowing air into your
uncooperative lungs. Perhaps, like more and more people, you
are spending your last moments in the twilight world of a cold
and sterile hospital, with tubes emerging from every natural ori-
fice and few unnatural ones, doctors and nurses hovering about.
Or perhaps you've just been gardening or golfing and one of the
blood vessels in your head has just disintegrated and down you
went, with a smile on your lips and earth under your fingernails.

Perhaps you are prepared, perhaps not. Oh well. Too late
now.

No matter what the cause, the surroundings, the company;
no matter what your bank account, your credit card, your paycheck; no matter what your beliefs, your deeds, your hopes,
fears, dreams—your time has come. You are dying, like every
other human being who has ever walked this earth. You are
going to meet your maker, sleep the big sleep, kick the bucket,
walk through the valley of the shadow of death, go to kingdom
come, join the ancestors, pass over.

But pass over to where? And how? And then what?

It's been said that religions exist mainly as a response to our
fears and questions about death and beyond. How do religions
try to fulfill their sacred mission to answer our questions and
calm our anxieties about our own mortality? What is death like?
Is there life after death? If there is, do we come back in other
bodies or do our disembodied souls live on in some spirit plane?
Are there things that we can do during our lifetimes to influence
what happens to us after we die? Can the still living influence the
fate of the deceased? And what about the big picture—is there a
larger cycle beyond our own short stay on earth in which the fate
of all of existence hovers?

For the most part, the original scriptures of the major religions are remarkably vague on details about the Great Beyond,

leaving much to the imagination and to subsequent literature. And what imaginations and literature we have when it comes to the afterlife! We have souls that fit into a thimble and grow to be eighteen inches long; souls that are separated from God, eat pus and are scorched by everlasting fires; souls that bask blissfully in the presence of the Divine, eat sweet fruits and are tended by beautiful youths and maidens; souls that rest in peace, or confer blessings or curses on their descendants; souls that are passed from one existence to another countless times; souls that are like blips in the unbroken, continuously fluctuating process of creation and destruction that is reality.

Many people presume—or fervently hope—that once we cross the threshold of death all our Big Questions Will Finally Be Answered and we'll know stuff like: Is there a God? What is God like? Is God a Being or a formless force? What is our relationship to God? Can we actually gaze upon the face of God, or is this a metaphor for an indescribable meeting and melding with the Ultimate? What is the meaning of life? What is the nature of reality? Maybe we'll get the answers to these questions, maybe not. Maybe we'll have answers to questions beyond our wildest imaginings.

JUST DESSERTS

The actual process of dying may be frightening and we may not want to leave our loved ones, but the possibility of life after death and partaking of this greater knowledge makes death itself a rather exciting proposition—unless you've been very, very bad. To be sure, our fear of death is part basic animal instinct for survival and part human terror of the unknown. But for many of us, what makes the little hairs at the back of the neck stand on end is the fact that religion tells us that the afterlife is the land of just desserts, the time and place where the wicked are finally punished and the virtuous are finally rewarded. Did you cheat on your income taxes, your spouse, your college exams? Did you toil thanklessly for civil rights, programs for the homeless, a cure for cancer? Were you cruel or kind? Honest or given to prevarication? Greedy and grasping or giving and generous? Did you believe in the Almighty?

The afterlife is an eternity that begins with a day of reckoning, the moment the cosmic yardstick appears to take the measure of our souls and determine our post-mortem milieu. We not only want the afterlife to exist because we can't conceive of being nonexistent; the afterlife *must* exist, if we believe in a just universe, because there is a dearth of justice during our earthly life. And think about it: if you were God, how would *you* keep unruly, imperfect Homo sapiens in line? Could you come up with a better deterrent than the stick of eternal horrific punishment for wrongdoing, or a better inducement than the carrot of infinite paradise to help us keep the faith during tough times?

But is this eventuality in fact better than the afterlife of ancient Mesopotamia, which mimicked earthly life in that there was no justice? Mesopotamian gods were cruel and capricious and dearly departed humans existed as "shades" doomed to float around the nether regions, no matter what efforts they made on earth. Are notions of spending eternity in heaven or hell preferable to the ancient Jewish assumption that death was final? Jewish afterlife did not acknowledge a distinct soul, but the spirit or breath of life did depart the body and all the dead existed, phantomlike, in a shadowy underworld that the Bible refers to as *She'ol*. This afterlife was dark and murky and not particularly pleasant, but it was equitable—saints and scoundrels all met the same fate.

At some point this murky beyond yielded to the concept of a soul and the afterlife became a more pleasant place, where one could have communion with God and loved ones. This was partly due to outside cultural influences and partly due to the need to reconcile the meaning of the covenant relationship between God and the Jewish people. The Hebrew Scriptures are vague on the subject, but the Bible does make tantalizing suggestions of an afterlife, particularly in the Psalms. Although still lacking in detail, these references implied a faith that death would not close the book on our existence. Judaism came to believe that the soul is released from the body at the moment of death. Or the soul hovers around until after the burial. Still another belief is that the soul remains in the body until the flesh actually decomposes.

In general, Jews do not obessess about the afterlife, ostensibly because God wants us to be active in realizing the Heavenly Kingdom here in this world. Why worry about something we know nothing about, and can do nothing about? As Irving Greenberg puts it in *The Jewish Way*, "Some religions seek to escape from our all-too-mortal daily round of life to the eternal presence of God. Judaism, conversely, seeks to draw the Divine into the world."

Christian doctrine, however, totally revolves around the immortality of the individual believer in Christ. Jesus died and was resurrected to redeem us, so that we too might have everlasting life and join God in the eternal bliss of his heavenly abode. Salvation is such a big message for Christianity that it is celebrated every Easter and every Sunday.

Judaism, Christianity and Islam tell us we are all judged personally by God, and that they also have a doctrine of the Divine will of God. This belief is especially strong in Islam, which says your fate—birth, death, damnation or salvation—is completely predetermined by Allah. After death, wicked and good souls alike undergo a trial, but since all has been predetermined it must perforce be a mock trial. That's the pesky conundrum when considering fair punishment and reward in this worldview: if all is predetermined, where is free will? How can a person change his ways from evil to good? How can we possibly be held responsible for our actions if they are by definition God's will? What reason would Muhammad have to urge people to change their ways and follow Islam? How could a loving, just and merciful God banish anyone to eternal punishment and damnation? Or even to temporary punishment, such as the purgatory of the Roman Catholic Church? It's just not fair.

For another take on spiritual justice we turn to Eastern philosophies, and the doctrine of reincarnation. Hinduism assumes that there is a soul that survives after death, and that the soul transmigrates to another body on earth. Life on earth is basically a preliminary to the life beyond; it is a series of reincarnations, and the circumstances of your life are determined by your actions in previous lifetimes. This is the natural law of karma, and it is automatic, impersonal—there are no personal deities to judge you—the universal moral and cosmic law of dharma determines all. If you have followed your dharma, you come back into a better position than in your last life; if not, you come back as a lowlier creature—which could be a plant, a bug, a parasite in a mouse's intestines, a bird or a streetcleaner. Buddhism holds similar beliefs of successive rebirths for the person who remains ignorant of the true nature of reality. Until that moment of enlightenment, karma dictates whether a person is reborn as a god, a human being, an animal, a hungry ghost or a denizen of heaven or hell.

This idea of a soul "coming back" or being "reborn" as someone or something else has resonated throughout history. While reincarnation is a curse in Eastern religions, it might also be seen as a second chance—to right previous wrongs, and to experience the growth necessary to meet a better fate. Jewish Kabbalists believed in the concept of the *gilgul*—the notion that a soul enters an earthly body to accomplish a "special mission" that helps her in her spiritual growth. At times she misses the mark, and is given another chance in another body, again and again, each time evolving in her knowledge of the Divine. According to this belief, Adam's soul was passed on to King David; Eve's soul entered Bathsheba; Abel was reincarnated as Moses.

Reincarnation or no, most religions offer ways to tinker with your fate: it's possible for humans or deities to intercede on your behalf. Your loved ones can pray, give you a proper burial, maintain the tomb and perform a variety of rituals designed to soften any punishment you may be meted. Muslims believe that the prophet Muhammad himself may intervene during the awesome judgment process. Roman Catholics believe that their friends and family may offer Masses, prayers and other acts of piety and devotion to shorten their stay in Purgatory. All Christians have Christ sitting at the right hand of God to nudge His father toward a more lenient verdict. Buddhists have the concept of the *bodhisattva*—someone who is moved by compassion to eschew the fruits of enlightenment until all sentient beings can enter nirvana, and who transfers his merit to those who need enlightenment. Tibetan Buddhist and Taoist priests perform funeral rituals to save the dead form harsh judgment and punishment in hell. And in China the practice of *feng-shui* helps make sure the deceased is buried in the most auspicious site according to the earth's energies, which will be channeled through the bones.

GOING, GOING, GONE

Death is both a process and an event that ultimately neither science nor religion can prevent. Scientists and theologians even have trouble defining death—not surprising, since there is no consensus on the definition of life. And that's another question for the theologians: is death the opposite of life—or part of it? When is a person clinically dead, and what happens on the spiritual plane?

We know generally, that corporeally speaking, at some point the heart stops beating, the circulation halts, the lungs cease breathing. Deprived of oxygen and nutrients, bombarded with toxic waste, your cells shrivel up or explode, blinking out like tiny lights. As dead cells pile up, organs and then entire organ systems begin to malfunction, including, most importantly, your brain. You may have an out-of-body experience in which you travel through a kind of tube toward a stunningly bright light and have a profound feeling of peace and acceptance. Scientists theorize that this image, described by many people who have had a "near-death experience," is a comforting hallucination brought on by a brain starved of oxygen, and is probably nature's way of easing our passage.

In any event, once the brain stem is no longer functioning and you are not capable of either breathing on your own or of having meaningful conscious thoughts and feelings, science pretty much agrees that you are irrevocably, irreversibly, incontrovertibly dead. Modern technology can keep your lungs inflating and deflating like a pair of balloons, your heart beating like a metronome, your cells nourished and cleansed—but on such life-support technology you are what is charmingly known as a "beating-heart cadaver." So it comes down to this: It is consciousness and respiration that constitute life on the material plane. On this science comes rather close to the age-old religious concepts of the soul and the breath of life as the animus of our being.

Ah, but what happens to the soul? And what is the soul, exactly? Do we really have one, or is this wishful thinking? Even before the known religions existed, Neanderthalers buried their dead in fetal position suggesting they believed that death was like a rebirth that thrust us—our souls—into the next world. The nature of the soul itself is rarely a simple concept. The early Egyptians believed a person was made of a complex collection of components: the physical body, a doppelgänger, a soul, a spiritual intelligence, power, shadow, a name and a metaphysical heart that was "the source of life and being" and which embodied thought, intelligence, memory, wisdom, sadness, bravery and love. In their divine obsession with death, these ancient people believed the soul could leave and enter the body, but could not survive without the physical body, which needed to be preserved at all costs, especially if it was a member of the royal family.

Hindus believe in a soul of sorts—it is called *atman* or the eternal, essential, unalterable self—which is said to be a mere particle of the cosmic consciousness. This atman is released from the body upon death; during cremation, the soul takes refuge in the head and the intense heat explodes the skull, which is said to help liberate the soul. In some Hindu traditions, the soul escapes through the nose, eyes and mouth. In a fascinating attention to detail, some Hindus believe that the soul of an intensely wicked person passes through the rectum, which causes it to accumulate such defilement that it requires endless purification in the hereafter. Buddhism's soul is a slippery concept: instead of the absolute self of Hinduism, it is the "no-self." This temporary blip of the cosmic consciousness that is constantly changing along with everything else in the universe—this nothing—nevertheless gets reborn, like the flame of one candle kindling the wick of another. Birth and death are merely interruptions in the fabric of ongoing creation and life process.

In the Jewish tradition, a person doesn't *have* a body, a person *is* a body and the spirit is blown into the flesh, and the combination is what makes for a whole person, a soul. Another view is that the soul comes from a storehouse in heaven, or from someone who once lived and died, and is incarnated or reincarnated.

As is to be expected, Christianity inherited Judaism's quicksilver concepts about the soul and afterlife. Christians once thought the soul resided in the liver—an organ for which no other purpose could be determined at the time. Some ancients thought its home was the heart; the brain was another possible seat of the soul. Some thought there were three souls—the "vegetative soul" in charge of autonomic body functions such as heartbeat and breathing, the "sensitive soul" whose domain was our reflexive reactions to the environment, and the "reasoning soul" which is what makes us rational beings and governs thought, judgment and responsibility for our actions. Whatever the location and nature of the soul, of one thing Christianity is certain: at death, the body starts to rot and the soul leaves immediately.

Islamic literature deals with creation, death, "life in the tomb," and our ultimate fate in graphic detail. These ideas are not based only on the Qur'an, but on subsequent writings, including *Kitab al-ruh*—"the Book of the Soul." Allah created humanity from clay and breathed His spirit into us. Each of us has a vital spirit or soul, the *nafs*, which is ours alone and is associated with rational consciousness. God takes away our souls when we sleep ("the little death") and when we die. According to the Qur'an, Allah "retains those against whom he has decreed death, but returns the others to their bodies for the appointed term." At the moment of the big death, the soul rises into the throat.

But once out of the body, where does the soul go? Where is the divine in the afterlife? Will we be able to see, hear, feel, touch, smell God or the gods? Is whatever is real or lasting in a person identical with the divine or different from it? When do our souls go to heaven, hell, or another place or person? How do we get there? How long do we stay?

ABODES OF THE SOUL

The souls of the deceased have intermediate destinations as well as ultimate destinies. Even Eastern religions have their versions of heaven and hell. In Hinduism, once the soul leaves the body, it enters a thumb-sized, vaporous container that is taken to Yama, the god of death. After Yama does a quick identity check, the soul returns to the home of the deceased, so it is crucial to perform the cremation before the soul comes back so it cannot reenter the body. The family and priest must carry out certain rituals of purification and respect so the disembodied, hovering soul (called a *preta*) can find a new home. They make ten balls of barley mixed with sugar, honey, milk, curds, clarified butter and sesame seeds and place them in a trench dug in a ritually purified stretch of land by a river. Together the priest and the son of the deceased perform rituals that symbolically create a head, neck, shoulders and so on, out of the barley balls and deliver the new entity, which is eighteen inches long, to Yama. This journey takes a year and is very perilous. After the soul completes it journey, Yama sentences it to a limited term in heaven or hell, according to what it deserves. It then is reincarnated into another body. In Hinduism heaven and hell are intermediate states in which the soul abides in between earthly lives. Your karma determines your passage through one of the seven levels of heaven or hell, which present varying states of suffering or bliss.

Hinduism actually presents two conflicting ideas about death. According to Rachel McDermott, assistant professor of Asian and Middle Eastern cultures at Barnard College,

> On the one hand, everyone would like to escape from the cycle of birth and death and reincarnation. But if you have not reached enlightenment, death means you will have to be reborn into a life that is inherently full of suffering. On the other hand, there is a more ancient idea that predates the concept of reincarnation. This other way of looking at death is much more "this world" oriented. Your survivors do a number of rituals designed to incorporate you, your soul, into the world of your ancestors.

Commemorative rituals are repeated annually, both to benefit the deceased and to cement their relationship with the living.

"From your relatives' point of view this is advantageous because you are available to them via prayer, and you intercede with the gods and can benefit them." However, if the rituals are not performed, or performed correctly, the preta may become a malevolent spirit.

The numerous schools of Buddhism posit various systems of multi-leveled heavens and hells. Each hell has its means of burning up the consequences of bad karma. The heavens offer various sensual and spiritual delights. The Pure Land Schools, common to Japan and China, describe a Paradise that is without pain and suffering, with beautiful natural surroundings of flowing rivers and lakes, pleasant music and exquisite gems. Chinese Buddhists say the yin aspect of your soul descends to a kind of purgatory to be judged and punished for evil deeds and set the level of incarnation into another life. Punishments are gruesome and physical and can last for eons. Finally, you get a cup of "the wine of forgetfulness" which wipes out all memory so you are reincarnated with a clean memory and again choose whether you will do good or evil on earth. But to end up in such places, or to be reincarnated on earth is to be a failure, because the aim in Hinduism and Buddhism is to be released from endless rebirths and to join with the Ultimate Reality.

In Judaism, once freed from the flesh, the soul goes to Gehenna, where it is judged and sentenced to punishment commensurate with the evil it had done while on earth. Maximum punishment is twelve months, hence the custom of saying the Kaddish for eleven months for your parents—long enough to be sure you've got them covered while in Gehenna, but not so long that you insult them by intimating that they were as evil as evil could be (which would require saying the Kaddish for twelve months). At the end of this period of punishment, the soul goes to "the end of time" or is put in storage until the end of time, or is reincarnated (interestingly, some say that being reincarnated and having to suffer through earthly existence again is Gehenna—a very Eastern notion). There is no notion of eternal punishment—only of eternal life or total oblivion. The Yiddish literature, however, has a fully developed hell akin to Dante's inferno.

There are almost as many versions of the afterlife in Christianity as there are churches. They do agree that heaven is a place of unimaginable rewards and bliss, and hell is place of unending punishment and torment—but this torment may simply be the absence of God. Most Christians believe the soul is immediately evaluated in a process called the Particular Judgment. But what is the standard of judgment? Some say a preponderance of good deeds over bad deeds will get you into heaven. Others say you must love God and accept Jesus as your savior, even if this happens one minute before you die after a life of horrible crimes against humanity. (Great humanitarians like Albert Schweitzer and Ghandi would not qualify, but a repentant Adolph Hitler and Stalin would).

Still others have elaborate criteria involving a state of grace and forgiveness of sins in the sacrament of penance. Once judged, you either go directly to your eternal reward in heaven, and God assumes the soul irreversibly and wholly into His Kingdom, or you are whisked away to hell, where you are tortured for all eternity. Or, you might go to Purgatory where your soul is systematically tortured with fire, but only temporarily, until it is cleansed of sin and worthy of heaven. Or still yet, you might enter a state of oblivion, unconsciousness, or unawareness, or a type of holding place similar to the She'ol of the Hebrew Scriptures or Hades of the Christian Scriptures and await a Final Judgment.

Orthodox Muslims believe that at the moment of death, the Angel of Death sits at the head of the deceased. According to the Book of the Soul, the angel tells "good and contented" souls to "depart to the mercy of God" and the soul leaves the body "flowing as easily as a drop from a waterskin." Angels wrap them in a perfumed shroud and are taken to the "seventh heaven" for record keeping and then returned to their bodies. Wicked souls, however, are told to "depart to the wrath of God." They are understandably reluctant to do this, and hide throughout the body, forcing angels to extract them "like the dragging of an iron skewer through moist wool, tearing the veins and sinews." These souls, exuding "the stench of a decomposing carcass," get wrapped in a scratchy hair-cloth. They, too, become part of the permanent record and are returned to their bodies. In Islam, unbelievers are tormented in their graves with heat and smoke from hell.

A BLINK IN THE MOTE OF GOD'S EYE

As an individual person, with feelings and fears and hopes and dreams, what happens to you after death assumes an importance of gigantic proportions. But really, in the larger scheme of things, the fate of the entire universe is the truly big question— if only because the fate of the universe will ultimately be the fate of your soul as well. Hinduism's worldview of time and exis-tence—and that of its major offshoot, Buddhism—is circular or cyclical and continuous. This vision of time and existence was most likely inspired by the regular and cyclical motion of the celestial bodies and recurring seasons. The linear view of time, characteristic of the Jewish tradition, and its offshoots, Christianity and Islam, see time flowing in a straight line that eventually comes to an end, and would be inspired by the obser-vation that all living things age and die, and that historical events happen once and impose permanent changes. These two views simultaneously influence ideas about the life cycle and afterlife of each individual human being as well as myths about the life-cycle of all existence.

In Hinduism, the wheel of birth and death—the cycle of birth, maturation, decay, death and rebirth—applies not just to the life

of an individual, but to the lifespan of a society and the course of
the entire cosmos. According to Hindu mythology, each world
cycle is divided into four world ages called *yugas*. As the cycle
revolves, the ages get progressively worse and more corrupt. *Krita
yuga* is the first, the purest and the best—a Golden Age. Men and
women are born virtuous and they devote their lives to fulfilling
their dharma. *Treta yuga* is less pure—evil is creeping in and order
is losing ground. As life begins to decay, people no longer perform
their duties spontaneously. *Dvapara yuga* is even worse. Human
beings are blinded by passion and lust after material possessions.
They grow mean and are reluctant to fulfill their sacred duties.
Kali yuga is the dark age. We are at our worst. According to the
text *Vishna Purana*, kali yuga is the age "where property confers
rank, wealth becomes the only source of virtue, passion is the sole
bond between husband and wife, falsehood the sources of success
in life, sex the only means of enjoyment" and outer trappings are
confused with religion. If this sounds familiar, it is because supposedly we are living in this age right now. Kali yuga "is rife with
all the problems that lead to the destruction of the earth," says
McDermott. "The world will disappear in a conflagration—
everything will melt back into Brahman. And then it will start up
again, when Brahman awakes."

When will this immense event occur? This present age is
said to have begun on Friday, February 18, 3102 B.C. and will
last a total of 432,000 years—so we are just over 5,000 years into
it, and have a little less than 427,000 years to go until the earth
disappears. If this seems like a long time, consider the fact that
dvarpana yuga survived twice as long—864,000 years; treta yuga
lasted three times as long—1,296,000 years; and krita yuga
extended for 1,728,000 years. The entire cycle is called *Maha
yuga*, and lasts 4,320,000 years. One thousand Maha yugas—
4,320,000,000 human years—is equal to a single day of
Brahman's time. The night is as long as the day, and during the

night, the god Vishnu sleeps on the serpent Ananta-Shesha, a symbolic reminder and embodiment of all the karma created by the last cycle. This karma will determine the form of the next cycle, just like a seed determines the form of a tree. At the dawn of the new day, from Vishnu's navel emerges a lotus, and from the lotus emerges Brahman, and from Brahman a new universe manifests to begin the cycle again.

This great cycle is contained within an even grander cycle, if you can believe it. At the end of Brahman's lifetime—100 Brahman years of Brahman days and nights—all spheres of being (not just the earth) are re-absorbed into the divine, primeval Substance. This quiescent state lasts for another Brahman century, and then the entire cycle of 311,040,000,000,000 human years begins all over again. Time measured on this scale is mind-boggling for the Western brain, which thinks that every 1,000 years (or less) the world is going to end. The earth may be a mote in God's eye, but a human millenium, which seems so vast, is not even a blink of Brahman's eye.

Religions that cling to a linear view believe the temporal world will simply come to the end of the road. But as is the case with an individual's life, the "end" is really the beginning. In this scenario, we have the vision of the Last Judgment and the final, great, consummating act of God. For Christians, this means the Second Coming of Christ, who will come down on the clouds of heaven in great glory. Christ will conduct the Final Judgement and the wicked will gather on one side, the righteous on the other, to hear the fateful words of welcome or banishment. Those who are already dead and have been judged will remain in heaven or hell. Those in purgatory will be released and moved to heaven. The bodies of the dead will be reconstituted which is called a body resurrection, and permanently reunited with their souls. All those who are alive at the time of the Second Coming will be judged and sent either to heaven or hell for all eternity.

Every "deliberate thought, word, deed, and omission" of every individual that has ever lived will be reviewed, which would include the entire life histories of the billions of people who have lived on earth for the hundreds of thousands of years that humans have been in existence. In this act, God intends to establish a heavenly society, a family of persons joined to each other and the holy trinity in everlasting knowledge, love and joy. You are reintegrated and given complete knowledge of and a place in God's total work.

At the End of Days according to traditional Jewish teachings, a Messiah will lead the Jewish people toward a time of peace and tranquility, a world without pain or evil, a world of perfection. On the day the Messiah arrives, history will end; the dead will be resurrected—the good ones and the ones who have been purged in Gehenna; the unredeemable will meet with eternal extinction. In Judaism, you don't have to be Jewish to attain "salvation." In the Jewish version of an afterlife, the doors to everlasting heavenly life are open to anyone who has lived an ethical life, a life of preponderantly good deeds. The Messianic Age will not come by itself—it will come "when we human beings have done what it takes to bring . . . perfection to our world. We don't sit and wait; we go out and act: for by the works of our hands, we bring glory . . . Each one of us must do his or her small part—creating, exploring, growing, participating, producing, repairing, healing, giving, caring, sharing, loving, transforming," writes Wayne Dosick in *Living Judaism*.

In Islam, the Day of Final Judgment resurrects both believers and nonbelievers, and both receive physical bodies to enjoy or suffer their final fate. The believers enter the Gardens of Delight. Martyrs of Islam have their evil deeds completely erased and they are sent to the Garden immediately. At the reception feast on the Day of Judgment nonbelievers fill their bellies with bitter fruit and proceed to hell, where they don "garments of fire" and have boiling water poured over them. Whenever their skins are too cooked to feel anything, they are given new skins so they may feel the punishment for eternity. Begging for annihilation and relief from the pain if this is your fate will get you nowhere; you are doomed to a living death.

ARE YOU READY?

But does any of this really help us face our own death with equanimity? Mother Teresa said, "If it was properly explained that death was nothing but going home to God, then there would be no fear." Is it really that simple?

Latif Bolat, singer of Sufi devotional songs, says, "The best example of how our philosophy helps you face your own mortality is the way we celebrate [the mystical poet] Rumi's death on December 17. The idea is that you are having a union with the Beloved by dying, so there is nothing to mourn. It is something to celebrate." Rumi himself said, "When you see my funeral procession . . . do not think that this is a separation, for it is my union with God."

Thomas Wolf, a singer who was raised as a strict Catholic, and who attended his mother's funeral last year, wonders why "everyone was quaking with spasms of grief—don't those people believe in God? Don't they believe in the resurrection and the life hereafter?" Belief in God and the certainty of joining Him in heaven is surely comforting to many people. But attending the funeral of a loved one is so hard because their death reminds us of our own mortality. It prompts us to ask, Why do we die? We might as well ask, Why do we live? Funerals make us wonder, Where do we go after we die? We might as well wonder, Where were we before we were born? Death is ultimately as mysterious as life itself.

Destruction is part of creation; death is part of life. If we are smart, we enjoy and celebrate and share the wonder and beauty and challenges of creation with others, while we are here. Because life is finite, death gives meaning and substance to our time here on earth, and to our relationships with others and with whom or whatever put us here. In dying, we are co-creators of the creation. As we return to dust and to the earth, we become the raw material for other forms of life. We make room for others, but live on in their memories; our good works reverberate through time like the ripples in a pond. Death is a portal into the next stage of our journey, even if that stage is only like a deep, deep sleep.

Those of us who have faced a life-threatening disease or near-death experience have learned the hard way to value the sweetness and tartness of life. If only we could achieve this wisdom without the painful shattering experience! If only we could hold onto this epiphany and not let it fade away. When it finally sinks in that life will one day be over and we don't have time to waste, we go back to the same question Rabbi Irvin Ungar asked at the beginning of this book: *How do you want to spend your time?* Pining away for some possible future paradise—or singing, praying, dancing, meditating, doing yoga, lighting candles, feasting, purifying, celebrating, mourning and enjoying and creating the treasure we have been given on earth?

Bibliography

Adams, Doug. *Dance as Religious Studies*. New York: Crossroad. 1990.

Barks, Coleman. *The Illuminated Prayer.* New York: Ballantine Books, 2000.

Bertman, Stephen. *Hyperculture: The Cost of Human Speed*. New York: Praeger, 1998.

Davies, J.G. *A Shaker Dance Service Reconstructed*. University of Birmingham: Institute for the Study of Worship and Religious Architecture, 1984.

Dossey, Larry. *Healing Words: The Power of Prayer and the Practice of Medicine*. New York: Harper, 1997.

Dosick, Wayne. *Living Judaism: The Complete Guide to Jewish Belief, Tradition, and Practice.* New York: HarperSanFrancisco, 1995.

Ellwood, Robert. *Alternative Altars: Unconventional and Eastern Spirituality in America.* Chicago: The University of Chicago Press, 1979.

Feuerstein, Georg. Yoga: The Technology of Ecstasy. New York: Putnam, 1989.

Fox, Rabbi Karen L. *Seasons for Celebration: A Contemporary Guide to the Joys, Practices, and Traditions of the Jewish Holidays.* New York: Perigee/Putnam, 1992.

Fox, Matthew. *Sins of the Spirit, Blessings of the Flesh.* New York, Harmony Books, 1999.

Friedlander, Ira. *The Whirling Dervishes.* London: Wildwood House, 1975.

Greenberg, Irving. *The Jewish Way: Living the Holidays.* New York: Simon & Schuster, 1988.

Gribetz, Jessica. *Wise Words: Jewish Thoughts and Stories Through the Ages.* New York: William Morrow and Company, 1997.

Halpern, Steven. *Sound Health: The Music and Sounds that Make Us Whole.* New York: Harper & Row, 1985.

Heschel, Abraham Joshua. *The Sabbath: Its Meaning for Modern Man.* New York: Farrar, Straus and Giroux, 1998 edition.

James, William. *The Varieties of Religious Experience.* New York: Penguin, 1985.

Kushner, Harold S. *When Bad Things Happen to Good People.* New York: Avon, 1981.

Merton, Thomas. *The Sign of Jonas.* New York: Harcourt, Brace and Company, 1953.

Milton, Ralph. *Christianity for Beginners.* Nashville: Abingdon Press, 1996.

Nelson, Gertud. *To Dance with God.* Paulist Press, 1987.

Orenstein, Debra. *Lifecycles: Jewish Women on Life Passages and Per-*

sonal Milestones (volume 1). Woodstock VT: Jewish Lights Publishing, 1994.

Praeger, Dennis and Telushkin, Joseph. *Nine Questions People Ask About Judaism*. New York: Simon and Schuster, 1981.

Roden, Claudia. *The Book of Jewish Food*. New York: Knopf, 1996.

Ronald Rolheiser. *The Holy Longing: The Search for A Christian Spirituality*. New York: Doubleday, 1999.

Ross, Lesli Koppelman. *Celebrate!: The Complete Jewish Holidays Handbook*. Northvale, NJ: Jason Aronson, Inc., 1994.

Roth, Gabrielle. *Sweat Your Prayers*. New York: Penguin, 1999.

Rybcynski, Witold. *Waiting for the Weekend*. New York: Viking, 1991.

Shaffer, Carolyn. *Creating Community*. New York: Perigee, 1993.

Smith, Huston. *The World's Religions*. New York: HarperCollins, 1991.

Somé, Malidoma Patrice. *Ritual: Power, Healing, and Community*. New York: Penguin, 1993.

Starhawk. *The Pagan Book of Living and Dying*. HarperSanFrancisco, 1997.

Tame, David. *The Secret Power of Music*. Rochester, VT: Destiny Books, 1984.

Thompson, Mel. *Eastern Philosophy*. Chicago: NTC/Contemporary Publishing Co., 1999.

Tucker, JoAnne and Freeman, Susan. *Torah in Motion*. Denver: A.R.E. Publishing, Inc., 1990.

Wall, Kathleen. *Rites of Passage*. Hillsboro, OR: Beyond Words Publishing, Inc. 1998.

Wouk, Herman. *This Is My God*. Boston: Little, Brown and Company, 1998.